In this book you wil

❑ A church, which d
shippers on many

❑ A village church doubling its membership in three years.

❑ A cinema, about to close because of poor business, being taken over for church services of 500 people.

❑ An Anglican church that holds the eucharist without a printed liturgy.

❑ A United church that increased its revenue by holding its annual budget campaign in the summer.

❑ A church charging ten dollars a seat for its sell-out Christmas Eve service.

❑ A church parking lot with space for more cars than the church used to have people.

❑ A church where Friday night is the biggest night of the week.

❑ A church with a youth program so big that its gym dwarfs its worship centre.

❑ A church whose Sunday offerings are large enough to need two armoured cars to pick them up on Sunday and Monday.

❑ A church that reserves pews for people who are "fragrance sensitive" and allergic to perfumes worn by other worshippers.

❑ A church where at one service, the pastor wore a Stetson hat when he gave the benediction.

❑ A church, started three years ago by a few friends in a small town, that has already planted a second one in another town and plans to start one in a third.

❑ A church that opened a new worship centre fully paid for without the members having contributed a single dollar.

❑ Some of these churches are in western Canada, some in central, some in eastern. Some are urban, some are rural. Some are old, some are new. Some are big, some are small. But every one of them is growing.

To my students
at Wycliffe College and the
Toronto School of Theology
1962 – 1997

"Growth is the only evidence of life."
John Henry Cardinal Newman
Apologia pro vita sua

Alive Again

Recession and Recovery
in the Churches

Reginald Stackhouse

Principal Emeritus and Research Professor
Wycliffe College, University of Toronto

Anglican Book Centre
Toronto, Canada

1999
Anglican Book Centre
600 Jarvis Street
Toronto, Ontario
M4Y 2J6

Canadian Cataloguing in Publication Data

Stackhouse, Reginald, 1925–
    Alive again: recession and recovery in the churches

ISBN 1-55126-257-6

1. Church renewal — Canada. I. Title.

BV600.2.S72 1999   262'.001'70971   C99-931208-1

Contents

There is now more good news than bad

This book is a good news story that reports how, after a generation of unprecedented recession, signs of a Christian recovery are now appearing in the northern sky. Most encouraging is the increasing number of growth churches in denominations that have been declining for three decades. To be found in all regions, environments, and communions, these growth churches show the way forward: what they have done, others can do, too.

This inspiring tale of renewal in Canada has its equivalents elsewhere. Throughout the United States, churches report dramatic growth — some of it astounding in scope, in numbers, and in imagination. From the Church of England has come a renewal program that has soared across both Atlantic and Pacific oceans to win enthusiastic response in other lands. What were marginal sects in many places just one generation ago have become strong denominations. As the Anglican Decade of Evangelism concludes and the Vatican calls for the year 2000 to be celebrated with outreach to the world, churches are becoming upbeat again.

Is it possible that this is false optimism? If this is not a time to whistle in the dark, neither is it a time to close our eyes to the light shining in the dark, a light that once again has shown that no dark can overcome it. It is a time to watch for the new day whose early rays assure us that the dawn is near. Although recovery is not yet here on a national scale, those with eyes to see can discern its coming.

In my research for this book, I travelled across the country to visit churches that have been growing. Funding limitations prevented me from visiting all the provinces and territories, and from studying growth in francophone and aboriginal churches. But this book does not purport to be an exhaustive work of social science. It is a theological witness to Christian growth. Its reports of growth in congregations of many different traditions tell us to be joyfully confident that a Christian revival is occurring among us right now. Instead of supplying statistics in graphs and charts, this book offers a picture of Christianity with a human face — one that is smiling again.

Acknowledgements

My appreciation for assistance with this book is offered to many people who are as much part of it as the author:

My wife, Margaret, not only for typing a major part of the manuscript, but for her encouraging interest in the project and her constructive advice.

The institutions whose financial assistance made the field research for this study possible: the Anglican Foundation of Canada, the Hellyer Foundation, the Jackman Foundation, and Wycliffe College.

Wycliffe College students who assisted with statistical and bibliographical research: Joan Bennett, Evelyn Fisher, Linda Robertson, and Shelly Tidy.

Peter Althouse, my teaching assistant, for thoughtful opinions, useful references, and personal cordiality.

Church leaders and clergy who offered relevant information and practical help:

The *Most Rev. Michael Peers*, Primate of the Anglican Church of Canada;

His Eminence, Aloysius Cardinal Ambrozic, Roman Catholic Archbishop of Toronto;

The *Most Rev. Percy O'Driscoll*, Anglican Metropolitan of Ontario;

The *Rev. Dr. Michael Pountney*, past Principal of Wycliffe College Toronto;

The *Ven. James Boyles*, General Secretary of General Synod, Anglican Church of Canada;

Monsignor Gregory Smith, Chancellor, the Roman Catholic Archdiocese of Vancouver; and

The *Rev. Canon A. Gordon Baker*, past Director of the Anglican Foundation of Canada.

The librarians and archivists of the University of Toronto, Emmanuel College, Knox College, Wycliffe College, the Anglican Church of Canada, and the United Church of Canada.

The clergy and laity who so cheerfully and graciously shared their time, information, help, and insight on church growth with me:

The Rev. Nick Brotherwood;
The Hon. Pauline Browes;
Margaret and James Bubar;
Pastor David Boyes;
The Rev. Brett Cane;
The Rev. Dr. Guy Chevreau;
The Rev. Earl Cooper;
The Rev. Paul Dempsey;
The Rev. Philip Der;
The Rev. Marcel Dubé;
Peter Dyck;
James Einfeld;
Laurene Einfeld;
The Rev. Dr. Maurice Flint;
The Rev. Peter Gillies;
Dawn Greer;
Dean Greer;
The Rev. Murray Henderson;
The Rt. Rev. William Hockin;

The Rev. Mark Hoogstein;

The Rev. Mike Horsman;

The Rev. Dr. Frank Humphries;

The Rev. Dale Huston;

Pastor Bill Klassen;

Dr. John Krahn;

The Rev. Douglas Jones;

Bishop Leon Lambert;

The Rev. Don Larson;

The Rev. Stephen Leung;

The Rev. Don Mann;

Pastor Phil Nordin;

The Rev. Dr. Barry Parker;

The Ven. Gary Paterson;

The Rev. Canon Barry Patrick;

Rachel Patrick;

The Rev. John Pentland;

The Rev. Canon Philip Poole;

The Rev. Robert Ripley;

Pastor Dan Sattelmaier;

The Rev. John Saynor;

Robert Shaw;

Allen Shaw;

The Rev. Paul Tang;

The Rev. Dr. Arthur Thompson;

The Rev. Richard Topping;

The Rev. Canon Clifford Ward;

Pastor Robert Weaver;

The Rt. Rev. Gary Woolsey; and

The Rev. Don Wright

Chapter 1

We live in a time of declining denominations and growing churches

It is old news that membership in Canada's historic denominations has been declining. The unreported good news is that across this vast country so many churches are advancing.

The negative message has been documented in best-selling books, trumpeted on national television, and proclaimed by communicators, some of whom seemed pleased about their reports of spiritual recession.

But that has been only half the story, the publicized half. The other half, the better half, deserves to be told, too. Without ignoring the negative, this book focuses on the new reality: the churches are growing again.

Since the 1960s, the so-called "mainline" denominations have undergone the most decimating challenge they have yet known in a land where, from the time of the first explorers until the seventh decade of this century, Christianity had been as much part of the national scene as the maple leaf.

When Jacques Cartier landed at Gaspé in 1534 to claim his discovery for Francis I, the Roman Catholic king of France, he erected a giant cross whose arms symbolically stretched over the Gulf of St. Lawrence toward the lands farther west. Almost half a century later in 1577, when Sir Martin Frobisher arrived at Baffin Island, his Anglican chaplain Master Robert Wolfall marked the occasion with a celebration of the Holy Communion as a thank-offering for the safe passage of the explorer and his crew across a hostile North Atlantic.

From the beginning of European settlement, Canada developed as a Christian country. Churches of all denominations became part of its landscape, and their traditions shaped the spirituality and morality of Canadian life. After the British conquest in 1759, the *canadiens* of Quebec survived as a people not only because they were allowed to retain their language, but also because they were given full freedom of religion. Their bishops and clergy filled the leadership void created when secular leaders returned to France and retained a leading role for 200 years.

Elsewhere, church extension paralleled colonial settlement as the country developed. Immigrants, mostly from Europe, were followed quickly by clergy and lay preachers who journeyed to the farthest reaches of the land. Missionaries defied a hostile nature to penetrate even the Arctic. By Confederation, Canada's identity as a Christian country was a stand-out feature.

In the century that followed, each decennial census showed both Roman Catholic and Protestant churches to have more members than they had claimed a decade before. Canada's parliaments opened with Christian prayers every day; great Christian festivals were public holidays; political leaders not only worshipped in churches but professed political values that had been shaped by Christian beliefs.

With a history like that, could anyone have criticized church leaders for assuming that the churches' growth and influence would go on forever? Who could have predicted the collapse of the '60's and the decades after them? Yet by 1991 as many as 3,300,000 Canadians told the census-takers that they professed "no religion." This group was the second-largest "denomination" in the land and the fastest-growing category.

Even the country's largest communion, the Roman Catholic, did not go untouched. Where over eight out of ten Roman Catholics told pollsters in 1946 that they had been to church in the previous seven days, just over one out of three made the same claim in 1990. The number of Canadians claiming to be Roman Catholic had risen during those years from 9,974,000 to 11,852,350, but the number of people on parish church rolls was smaller than these census totals, and the number of people regularly attending mass smaller still.

Between the mid-1960s and 1970s, an unprecedented exodus of clergy and nuns left their ministries, leaving vacancies yet to be filled. Every year more clergy die than are ordained, and the age level of the pastoral clergy has become impracticably high. In spite of underused seminaries being closed, the remaining theological centres are not at capacity.

Nowhere has the shock been felt more deeply than in Quebec, the once apparently impregnable fortress of Roman Catholicism. Although the eighteenth-century Enlightenment and French Revolution had undermined the church in France, Quebec escaped these upheavals, and continued to build its culture on the threefold foundation of religion, family, and land. Then, with the abruptness of an earthquake, the "Quiet Revolution" of the 1960s tore apart Quebec's unique seventeenth-century mode of life, and the province became every bit as secular as the rest of the country, in some ways more.

Before the 1960s, almost nine out of ten Quebec Roman Catholics went to church at least twice a month. Just two decades later, the number had dropped to four out of ten. Vocations for the priesthood and the convents were slashed. The birth rate fell from the highest on the continent to the lowest in the country, despite Roman Catholic teaching on birth control. Education was transferred to the authority of a provincial department of education. A human rights code was adopted that was ahead of the rest of Canada. Between the 1981 census and the 1991 census, the number of Quebeckers professing to have "no religion" almost doubled.

Decline has been more devastating still among the once-strong Protestant denominations that look back on centuries of tradition and on having been a fundamental part of Canadian life for so long.

The country's largest Protestant denomination, the United Church of Canada, formed only in 1925, traces its ancestry to the sixteenth-century Reformation through the Presbyterian and Congregational components in the denominational merger that created it. The other component, the Methodists, were descended from the eighteenth-century Evangelical revival. All three communions had been strong, and when their historic merger took place, this old/new denomination was soon found everywhere. It grew steadily, and its leaders were heard with respect, especially on social issues, its membership peaking in 1966 at 1,062,000. But by 1985 it, too, had dropped — all the way to 881,000.

Other historic denominations were hit hard at the same time. About one-third of the Presbyterians had voted to remain out of the United Church of Canada in 1925, and to carry on as the Presbyterian Church in Canada. It grew in strength slowly until in 1961 membership totalled 202,566, but by 1985 the number was only 153,928.

Canada's Lutheran population had expanded through immigration from Germany and Scandinavia as well as the United States. Although some of the constituent bodies that in 1986 joined to form the Evangelical Lutheran Church in Canada continued to grow modestly until then, overall numbers remain fairly constant at about 200,000.

Baptists are not formed into a national denomination: autonomous congregations join together in conferences and conventions, organized on the basis of region or doctrinal position. A modest downward trend was found among them during these years, from 137,000 in 1966 to 130,000 in 1985.

The country's third-largest denomination, the Anglican Church of Canada, had grown partly as the result of immigration from the British Isles and parts of the world influenced by Anglican missionaries. Anglican numbers had risen steadily since 1893 when the scattered dioceses of Canada had been gathered together under the authority of a General Synod. But from a high of 1,359,601 in 1965, Anglican numbers collapsed by 37% to 848,256 in 1991.

Just as critical as numerical decline for these denominations was the aging of the members who remained. Not only were there fewer worshippers in the pews, but also there were so few young people among them that institutional demise appeared imminent. The causes were many: a lower birth rate, a more mobile lifestyle, indifference among the younger generation to denominational loyalties. But the result was inescapable: there were fewer heads in church, and those present were mostly gray.

Dropping Sunday school enrolments were another alarming sign: churches without children and young people were churches without a future. Enrolment in United Church Sunday schools fell from a high of 765,855 in 1960 to 207,758 thirty years later. Anglican numbers declined 35% between 1972 and 1990. In the '70's and '80's, Presbyterian registrations slid from 63,362 to 33,698, and enrolments in Sunday schools of the Lutheran Church-Canada (one of the original Lutheran bodies) were cut from 27,568 to 13,584.

This decline in membership of Canada's religious establishment was all the more dramatic when contrasted with what had been happening in evangelical sects, once small in membership and marginal in status. Their numbers zoomed up. They erected impressive worship centres, maintained professional quality media ministries, opened Christian schools, and grew at about the same rate at which the historic denominations were declining.

Even a few examples can impress anyone who has read only about decline. The combined Pentecostal Assemblies of Canada and of Newfoundland grew from 155,000 members in 1972 to 226,691 in 1990. The Christian and Missionary Alliance increased from 22,783 in 1972 to 80,681 in 1992. The Seventh Day Adventists went from 21,434 to 42,083 in the same period, and the combined Mennonite membership leaped from 47,149 to 79,446. Other evangelical communions achieved comparable expansion, so that by the 1990s, their combined totals of more than a million adherents represented a significant portion of the Christian population.

No longer were these groups marginal. And their arrival as a spiritual force showed that "reverse" was not the only gear Canadian Christians could use. In an age of decline, growth was possible.

It began to appear in the traditional denominations as well. Startling growth was achieved by some congregations, even during the years when their denominational totals were dwindling. The number of these growth churches has not yet been enough to offset the reductions in each declining denomination, but their pattern of growth is being observed by more and more clergy and laity who now believe that decline can be reversed. Recovery is open to those who seek it.

This book is about churches that have sought and found growth. Their experience offers a model for others. Incredibly diverse in every way, they are found in all denominations and regions. Some are massive, some minuscule. Some are traditional, some contemporary. Some are liturgical, some free-form. In some places, longstanding churches have become revitalized. Elsewhere, new churches have emerged almost full-grown. Some have expanded to memberships in the thousands; for others, growth has meant 25 worshippers on Sunday instead of 20. But all share one characteristic: they are growing.

That to achieve growth they have followed a common pattern is the chief message of this book. If each growth church were unique, if its style and content were inimitable, this book would offer little aid and comfort. The good news is that most growth churches follow a methodology that others can adopt.

The pastor does not have to be a superstar with Charlton Heston's voice, Barbra Streisand's stage presence, or Tom Cruise's sex appeal. Neither do a church's lay leaders have to be the elite of their community, rich in talent, time, and re-sources. Any church can attempt growth — and succeed. By reading the story of these churches that have been successful, even the gloomiest of prophets will recognize that it is not yet "game over" for Christianity in Canada.

Chapter 2

Within every church there is a growth potential praying to get out

Port Carling, Ontario, may not seem a likely place to find a growth church, one dynamic enough to double its attendance, enlarge its building, and pay for this construction — all in three years, all without a population increase, all following hard on an economic recession. But that is what happened in this picturesque village in a Precambrian shield cottage region within easy driving distance of Toronto.

Knox Presbyterian is one of three churches serving the year-round residents who live where the Indian River links two of the majestic Muskoka lakes. Throughout the holiday season, the Port is alive with vacationers who come by boat and car to taste its beauty and revel in the contrast to big-city life. But most of the year, it does not bulge with weekenders, vibrate with shoppers, bounce with coffee-shop "rock." In the off-season it seems the last place to draw an ambitious young minister filled with energy and enterprise.

Yet that is precisely what it did in 1993 when Knox Church called the Reverend Richard Topping and his wife, Amy. Rick and Amy found a church whose normal Sunday attendance ranged from 20 to 30 and rose to 60 or 70 during the summer cottaging months. One teacher was staff enough for a Sunday school of five children.

When the Toppings left three years later, regular attendance had doubled to 40 or 60, and on summer Sundays, 90 to 100 crowded into the church. Thanksgiving Sunday in October made it bulge with an overflow of 130. The Sunday school kept pace, too, increasing in the summer months to between 15 and 30 children. Many worshippers not only attended but joined, thus increasing Knox's membership from 36 to 52. The number of adherents grew until the mailing list held over 100 addresses. To add a minister's study cost $35,000, and the money was in hand before the work was begun.

Those numbers may not seem impressive when put up against those of the country's great churches, like Montreal's St. Andrew's and St. Paul's Presbyterian, where Rick and Amy moved when he became its assistant minister. But when they are translated into percentages, they are phenomenal. They remind us that church growth can be found in villages as well as metropolises. They also remind us that growth need not involve a TV superstar celebrity preacher. Nor an offbeat religious experience. Growth can be the big feature of the little church around your corner.

Growth was a feature of an even smaller church where Rick and Amy also served while in Port Carling. Zion Church in nearby Torrance was a case for closure by 1993. Its regular attendance was six people out of a membership of 13. In the summer, attendance soared to 15 or 20. Significantly, there was no Sunday school. By 1996, however, Zion was growing more than Knox in percentage terms: 17 on regular Sundays and summer numbers of 35 to 50. Church membership grew to 25, and a Sunday school was formed for 14 children with three teachers. Where total revenue in 1992 had been $17,418.68, by 1995 it had become $23,384.22.

"But what about spiritual growth?" people ask. Simple answer: if big numbers do not indicate real faith, neither do small ones.

But numerical growth and spiritual vitality can go together. At Zion Presbyterian, worship was enriched by two superb musicians devoting their talents at the organ and piano. Zion also produced its own song book to serve a now ecumenical congregation not familiar with the denomination's hymns. Holy Communion was celebrated once a month instead of quarterly. Visual aids increased the impact of sermons. When the exchanging of the Peace was introduced, so great was the enthusiasm that it sometimes took five minutes to complete.

This fellowship note resounded throughout the weeks, too. A telephone directory of members and adherents was assembled and a quarterly newsletter distributed. Rick visited each member twice a year, and called on all Torrance people in hospital, whether they were churchgoers or not.* An annual pot luck supper brought everyone to the manse for an evening with Rick and Amy. Men's breakfasts on Saturday drew capacity attendances. And all this was without the histrionics of a glitzy, slick Hollywood style, or without a massive megacity population to draw from.

In these two small churches there was a growth potential — and growth potential can be found in churches right across the

* The minister now is Mark Hoogstein.

country. It can be found in churches in isolated rural communities as well as in fashionable suburban ones, in declining denominations as well as in booming ones, in traditional or innovative congregations, in churches that reach out to family-oriented neighbourhoods or draw singles with unmet spiritual needs.

How do these diverse churches turn challenge into opportunity? Let us look at four types of growth as we visit churches right across Canada.

1. Expanding Growth

Expanding growth occurs when small numbers become bigger as a result of the church's ministry.

During an election, a campaign manager may revise the strategy in order to give a lagging campaign a "bounce." That is close to what happened when Dan Sattelmaier assumed a very ordinary neighbourhood pastorate on the edge of Regina in 1978, made it bounce into being one of the largest Lutheran churches in the west, and kept it bouncing until he concluded his ministry there in 1998. In those years a smallish congregation showed what can happen when a church accepts expansion as one of its goals, and although Dan has now accepted another call, the impact he had will be felt for a long time.

Celebration Lutheran may be like no other Lutheran church you have ever attended. Everything about it seems different. Even the Renfrew Crescent parking lot with capacity for 150 vehicles is much larger than the space most churches provide. But Celebration recognizes that people will drive a long way to a church they like if they can park easily when they get there.

With its octagonal shape and glass doors, the church does not look like a typical place of worship. The ethos is distinctive too. You enter a spacious reception area large enough to hold 200 people, and before you have read even a few of the numerous notices, you are greeted by an usher. He does it so well that when you compliment him, he reveals that he makes a specialty of welcoming newcomers. Communicating may be a specialty of the whole church, you think, when you notice a bank of mail slots, one for each family or individual, where members can pick up their church notices postage free.

It must be working, you infer as you walk into the sanctuary, because half an hour before service time, 33 adults are there in a class being taught by the pastor. This worship centre has all the traditional chancel equipment — candles, cross, altar, font, organ — but it does not seem traditional. A five-piece band assembles together with four singers, three women, and a man who also announces the songs (as he calls the hymns), introducing them with brief homilies on praise and thanksgiving.

By now the adult class has been joined by a steady inflow of worshippers, and the pastor, who has exchanged his gray suit for a white alb, is playing the organ as the people join in a singalong prelude to the service. Soon the place is bouncing, everyone singing words projected on a large screen lowered from the ceiling. Well before 11 o'clock, all but two of the 500 chairs are filled by people who have come to sing, and a Grade 12 student reveals that he was brought first by a friend but now comes on his own because he likes the music. Others obviously do, too: some clapping, some raising their hands, some standing up, some swaying from side to side, everyone participating.

At 11 o'clock, the pastor speaks briefly about a supernatural power being at work in the worship and then returns to the organ while a music director leads us in another four songs. One is a familiar psalm, but the tempo is so different that the words seem new, too. By now there is enthusiasm in the air and when the Peace is exchanged, some move into the aisles to greet others, some embrace one another, and almost a din of fellowship is heard.

The sermons at Celebration are traditional in content but contemporary in style. Dan once preached a whole year on the lordship of Christ and the next year on the Holy Spirit. Sometimes he reinforces his message by showing a video that drives it home.

When Dan arrived in 1979, there were 70 adults in the congregation and 15 children in the Sunday school. Things began to grow, and by 1995 when the church moved into a new and much larger building, average weekly attendance was 730.

Actual membership is now 450, plus a host of adherents who come regularly but do not wish to join. The annual budget is $504,000, including payments on the $1,600,000 building debt — an astronomical rise from the $14,000 budget of Dan's first year, when the church needed a subsidy from the denomination to stay open.

To keep it all bouncing, Dan was assisted by three other pastors for youth and young adults, Christian outreach (including small groups), and children's ministries. The appointment of a music minister was next. In addition, there are two secretaries and a part-time caretaker.

But how has all this expanding growth happened? Regina itself has grown, but church expansion does not automatically keep pace with population growth or, as in this case, exceed it.

The explanation must start with Dan himself. He brought to his people what he calls "a vision of growth" that he has helped to make real by his strong emphasis on scriptural preaching and teaching. Describing himself as "Lutheran in doctrine, evangelical in focus," he favoured a charismatic worship style as part of a ministry he said is "Holy Spirit empowered."

But no one person can do it all. Dan's ministry was enhanced by others, especially his wife, Darlene, who was on the church staff for some time, as well as a specialized pastoral team and an army of volunteers. The program needs an army. Six volunteers are required just to operate the audio-visual equipment for Sunday worship. Laity also pastor one another through more than 40 "care groups," each involving from four to 15 persons who share a program of mutual caring, reaching out to others, and studying the scripture. Most meet in homes, but one meets at an office. A Working Women's Fellowship meets at lunch hour once a week. A Grief Group enables the bereaved to minister to one another.

Special Sunday services focus on particular persons and needs. A "Teacher Appreciation Sunday" gave each child a chance to invite a day-school teacher to worship at the church, and the 30 who came each received an apple. "A Marriage Renewal Sunday" brought out 35 couples, and 200 attended a seminar for abused women.

Dan told me that to keep growing, the church needed additional services, such as a second Sunday morning service — one for people not attracted by the worship style now offered at 11 o'clock. He also hoped to build a gymnasium, increase the staff, and launch a two- or three-year stewardship campaign.

Even the church's name suggests the future. Like so many other growth churches around the world, this one dropped its old area designation, Glen Elm, in favour of one with an upbeat message: Celebration. But its name also tells people its denomination: Celebration Lutheran.

Both names are needed to describe it. On the one hand, the congregation includes people of many church backgrounds or none at all, 60% not having been active in any church for the previous five years. Many of them want to leave it that way, happy to belong to this church but not willing to join its denomination. Yet the church is Lutheran, Dan himself being a third-generation Lutheran pastor. The church could not have achieved what it has without Lutheran backup; its building project was made possible with a denominational loan of $1,200,000.

In this dual character, however, Celebration Lutheran is part of a new trend. It is no longer possible to assume that most people will stay with the tradition in which they were reared as children. Ideas and inspiration also come from beyond denominational boundaries. Dan, for example, went as far as California to learn new and better ways from a pastors' conference at Robert Schuller's Crystal Cathedral in Garden Grove, California.

Yet congregations still need to be part of something larger than themselves. Churches can now grow beyond denominations without separating from them. Knox Church, Port Carling, and Zion Presbyterian, Torrance, are other examples of the same trend. Growth is changing the relationship that historically could be assumed.

That is not the only change we discover in a trip east to the Atlantic region. At Hartland, New Brunswick, you cross the historic St. John River on what is advertised as the longest covered bridge in the world. But if you drive inland from the river to the village of Coldstream, you can find something even more distinctive: its United Baptist Church may be the only congregation in Canada to build a gym larger than the worship centre.

Why have they done it that way?

The explanation does not imply any downgrading of spirituality but an upgrading of its regard for young people. Children and youth from kindergarten to college age, 120 strong, belong to its AWANA program: A Workman And Not Ashamed. The youngest children come on Monday afternoon after school, and the rest assemble Tuesday evening. On Sundays, they are back for church and Sunday school.

Coldstream United Baptist may also be unique for a second reason. It just may be the "buildingest" church in the country, with an astounding construction program that since 1987 has seen a new parsonage erected, followed by the big gym, and then a new church. Sunday attendance had so outgrown the old one that a larger sanctuary seating over twice as many worshippers became a necessity.

Does this expansion result from the Atlantic region's being the "churchiest" part of Canada? Not when we realize that a nearby United Baptist congregation had become so small that it had to close its church after generations of service. There are other reasons why Coldstream has grown the impressive way it has, reasons that can remind us of the churches we visited in Ontario and Saskatchewan.

One of them is the Reverend Mike Horsman, whose arrival in 1987 began the building program that has scarcely paused since. He is universally respected as the human dynamo in this church's power plant, a pastor who seems to do everything well — preach, teach, counsel, organize. But ability is not all that he has brought to Coldstream.

As one of his people put it, he makes everyone feel "special." This quality builds relationships in the church as well as the community, where everyone knows him as Mike and where he is as welcome with the men who gather for coffee in the general store as he is with the Women's Missionary Society.

Mike has done something else that's very important. Where the church had suffered from a turnover of previous pastors who came and went, he has stayed — and gives no sign of wanting to leave in spite of opportunities having come his way. Long tenures have become a feature of expanding churches and others that enjoy growth. When pastor and people come together in a partnership that makes for progress like the kind Coldstream church has enjoyed, no one wants it to end.

But stellar as its pastor is, this church has other vital assets. Its people are apostolic in their commitment, 15 of its members contributing 20% of their incomes to sustain the pace of the work. Two senior members, Margaret and James Bubar, testify to their hope that the Lord will spare them long enough to see the church free of debt.

Participation is another feature of this lively church. When a newcomer enters the church's spacious reception area, he is welcomed by two greeters who learn his name. This simple act is all the more striking because most of the people in the community have known each other for years, some for a lifetime, and could easily be so absorbed in one another that they could forget "the stranger within the gates." But they do not.

The sanctuary is traditional in design and furnishing, and the order of worship is traditional, too. But there is plenty of personality. When the service begins with a singalong, people request favourite hymns. Then a soloist is invited to come to the front and sing, "I will hold on to the hand of my saviour." The offering is collected by ushers who include young people just as serious about their commitment as their elders. During the sermon, the preacher's frequent scriptural references are accompanied by the swishing sound of people turning the pages of their Bibles to look them up themselves. At one point, worship is recessed, so that everyone can greet the person beside him or her and say: "You look great and I'm really glad you're here." At Coldstream worship is not loose, but it is not impersonal.

Here is a church that is growing because its people matter to each other, matter enough that the mid-week prayer meeting divides into groups of two, so that each person can make prayer requests of the other without losing privacy.

Mike and the Coldstream congregation are a winning combination that can tell "wannabe" growth churches something worth learning.

2. Sustaining Growth

Sustaining growth attracts enough members to equal the inevitable loss a congregation must suffer each year.

Church growth, however, means not only raising numbers but sustaining them, and maintaining growth is no less a challenge than beginning it. Churches cannot avoid losing members through death, illness, removal, and myriad other causes. Some estimate this attrition to be as high as 20% a year. These losses must be replaced if a church is to retain its human strength.

Two churches in downtown Montreal are examples of sustaining growth in spite of the anglophone flight from Quebec for the past quarter-century. One of them, Evangel Pentecostal, stands across the street from the old Forum hockey arena, but while the national sports shrine has closed, the church is thriving. Every Sunday, 950 people fill the church, 650 in the morning and 300 in the evening. On a special occasion such as Mother's Day, 700 can turn out in the morning, and 500 come for the evening Spring Festival of Music. Evangel is not just holding its own; it is doing better than ever, with attendance averaging more than 100 above what it was in the early 1990s.

How does evangel do it? As a denomination, the Pentecostal Assemblies of Canada have grown since 1965, but many Pentecostals have fled the inner city to the more congenial suburbs. Why has Evangel stayed and thrived?

Part of the explanation lies in its readiness to adjust to new situations. As senior pastor, the Reverend Don Mann is at ease with Montreal as a multicultural city. His congregation can include people from 40 different countries on any given Sunday. He makes the most of this by developing ethnic fellowships, such as a Filipino one that may become large enough to form a church of its own, as well as comparable Nigerian and Ethiopian groups. So prominent is this feature of Evangel that a Week of Missions was started by a Parade of Nations Sunday, when 42 national flags were carried into the church, each representing a country from which some of the worshippers had come.

Newcomers are not only given a welcome by a host and hostess, but are also invited after church to a reception where Don and his wife, Marie Jose, assure them that though they came as visitors, they leave as friends. They are also given a box of cookies to take with them, and during the week they receive a welcome letter. Lay visitation later follows as part of a program that in 1997 contacted 500 people.

But holding onto the newcomers after welcoming them is another priority at Evangel. Don wants to "slow down the revolving door" through which as many people may leave a church as enter. He hopes that a discipleship instruction program will help meet this need by providing people with teaching that can lead to spiritual maturity and keep newcomers from falling away. The church's ministry is enhanced also by a strong and popular music program involving three choirs with 90 singers under a part-time music director. A youth pastor makes sure that young people's needs are met. A "True Love Waits" program, for example, attracted 40.

The church's work has been expanded with the acquisition of an adjacent building that will not only hold administrative offices but will also provide space for a banquet hall. It is singularly well equipped for that purpose because it was formerly the location of two restaurants. Now it will increase the church's capability of feeding people as a dimension of their fellowshipping together, such as on a Family Fun Day, when over 900 hot dogs were served.

Dynamic as Evangel is, its ministry is not unique. A short ride on the Métro takes us to another church also thriving in downtown Montreal, in spite of the dramatic social changes the city is experiencing. The People's Church, too, has refused to move; in fact, it has enlarged its facilities, so that it can better serve the over 350 who gather each Sunday. The senior pastor, Dr. Frank Humphries, and the members reason that their central location across from McGill University is a "must" because the church draws people from all over the island of Montreal. On Sundays traffic is not a problem, nor is parking, because the church pays the costs at the next-door parking garage.

Clearly, this church is successful at sustaining itself partly because it adjusts its way of doing things to meet the needs of its people. Although most churches schedule their programs throughout the week, People's does just the opposite. It holds its congregational activities all on the same night — Friday. Why? It would be impossible for most families to drive different members downtown several nights a week. Frank also reasons that it would be wrong to fracture the family life the church wants to strengthen. When all the groups meet on the same night, they use up all the available space at the church, but the church rents rooms and a gym in a nearby high school and enjoys the use of a boardroom in an adjacent office building.

The approach is working so well that a second Sunday morning service has become necessary, and the church has spent $240,000 on a renovation program to increase its building's usefulness. It is an impressive record, especially when one learns how a nearby Protestant church that once boasted 2,500 members had to close after declining to 50.

At People's Church, as in other growth churches, good pastoring is central. Like Mike Horsman at Coldstream United Baptist in New Brunswick, Frank is in for the long term. He has been in this pastorate since 1978 and does not dream of faraway pastures. A McGill Ph.D. graduate, he does most of the preaching and much of the pastoring of sick people, but to make the ministry all the stronger, an associate pastor, Martin Good, looks after administration and pastoral counselling and helps conduct the worship.

To strengthen the church's outreach to people in nearby neighbourhoods, the pastoral team also includes a Director of Outreach, Tony Schaapman. As a full-time missionary for Open Air Campaigners, he is posted to People's to give leadership with such ministries as the regular weekly door-to-door visitation in the neighbourhood by pastors and laity. These visitations are not high-pressure evangelism; the visitors leave literature that tells what goes on at People's and invite people to come.

This inner-city congregation is growing at a time when it could be dying. But it is not unique. Much of what it does can be found elsewhere. Let's journey west again to see what others are doing.

If we stand outside Hillsdale Church in Regina on any Sunday, we will see people who could be going into any church anywhere in Canada. Some are old, some young, many in between. Most come by car. Most are dressed as if for an occasion. Most look comfortably well off.

But there is one difference: there are so many of them — over 900! Hillsdale is known throughout the west as one of the Christian and Missionary Alliance's strongest churches. The achievement is all the more notable when we learn it has maintained these numbers for years.

It was not that way at the beginning in 1928 when Hillsdale began humbly in rented space at a Royal Canadian Legion hall and then at the Order of the Moose. But a year later the church built its own hall and then expanded to include a chapel in 1932 and a tabernacle in 1939. There it stayed until further growth demanded the present distinctive edifice be built, with its unique "praying hands" shape, to seat 650. That was in 1967, when church attendance in Canada was in a free fall, and it might have seemed a demonstration of Cyril Parkinson's law that buildings are often erected after the need for them has passed. But it was not that way with Hillsdale. Since 1967 it has shown how impressive sustaining growth can be.

Leadership is a major reason why. Hillsdale's multifaceted program is directed by a professional staff that, as well as the senior pastor, includes pastors for adults, youth, children, women, and music. There are also two part-time pastors for university students and visitation. Leadership also includes the laity, and not just on the fringe. When the senior pastorate was vacant and no associate had been in office for long, the role was assumed by one of the church members. Peter Dyck, a retired senior official of the Department of Education in Saskatchewan, undertook the task of coordinating both pastoral and administrative staffs, so that there would be no break in the church's ministry.

His kind of leadership capability is not unusual in a church where half the members have had post-secondary education, 40% do professional work, and almost two-thirds are in the upper-middle or upper-income brackets. But there is more to Hillsdale's lay leadership than social composition. The laity are encouraged rather than stifled. The stress is on participation, the key words on church literature and posters being "In Touch." The objective is for people of every age group, from young children to senior citizens, to keep in touch with each other and to help one another keep in touch with the Lord.

So, as soon as you enter the spacious narthex, you are greeted by the first of four ushers who make you welcome before you leave. Hillsdale esteems each person so much that it may be the only church in Canada to take account of the special needs of people with allergies. It reserves some pews as "fragrance free," and ushers escort worshippers with strong perfume or after-shave away from these seats. That unusual bit of sensitivity shows what being in touch with people's needs can mean.

The church's facilities are now so taxed, Peter Dyck explains, that teachers have had to caution their pupils against inviting their friends to come with them. "That should not be the way a church thinks," he comments, adding that two morning services are now required to accommodate regular attendance. The time for a still larger sanctuary has come. Hillsdale will be led in this $4-million building campaign by its new senior pastor, the Reverend Gordon Grieve, who has already inspired his people to see growing as part of their caring.

Caring characterizes growth churches as we can discover by travelling farther west. In Calgary, you have only to walk into St. Peter's Anglican to learn why it has sustained its growth — it is a people place.

When you enter, you may see adults rehearsing a major drama production or teenage girls on their way home from a weekly meeting. You may see men and women on a spiritual quest at an adult baptism and confirmation course. Or you may happen on a monster-size event like the annual Calgary Stampede Sunday Morning Service And Pancake Breakfast.

St. Peter's is an example of a program church, too large for the "I know everyone" intimacy of a small congregation but not ready to turn itself into a "bulk religion store." Instead it stimulates fellowship through a variety of groups and events in which everyone can find a place. Sunday worship, too, serves human diversity by including a service for those who prefer the *Book of Common Prayer* and one for those who want a more contemporary liturgy.

Keeping it all going is a full-time task for two full-time clergy, and Bishop Gary Woolsey, the rector, is lucky to have even one day in seven free from the demands of his 500-family membership.

But full as the church's life is, the bishop and his lay leaders are always seeking more. The church recently spent $7,000 for an illuminated sign to communicate more effectively with the more than 10,000 people who drive or walk past it every day of the week.

Newcomers are welcomed from the chancel at each Sunday service, and their names and addresses are obtained at a table set up for them in the narthex after the service. Over coffee they have a chance to meet the clergy and some of the laity. Twice a year, new members are invited to a get-together when the clergy and lay officers tell them about St. Peter's. In every way they are welcomed and made to feel at home.

But growth can never be static and a church that stands still soon finds itself sliding backwards. A large church like St. Peter's loses parishioners every year and sustains itself only by involving people in fellowship that opens its heart and its door to everyone.

Like Don Mann at Montreal's Evangel Church, Gary is concerned about a dimension of sustaining growth that receives too little attention: reaching people who have dropped out of church, who for some reason or other have just stopped coming. It is very easy in a large church for a person to miss services without anyone noticing, and if this absenteeism continues beyond six months, it can be difficult to recover the old commitment. Yet few churches have a ministry to the lapsed. If they did, sustaining growth would be easier.

3. Cyclical Growth

When growth in numbers occurs as a result of a demographic change, it may be cyclical growth.

Cyclical growth can sweep up a small church and carry its membership to numbers no one had ever expected. It most often occurs in suburban communities and commuter towns near expanding cities, but it happens, too, in small towns and villages when there is an ingress of retirees and ex-urbanites wanting to get away from big-city life. Another form of cyclical growth occurs when immigrants of the same ethnic origin seek community with one another in the same church.

It would be easy for a church to sit back and wait for the people to roll in. But the cycle of population growth in a community translates only into potential church growth. To transform that potential into actual growth, the church has to capitalize on it, the way our next church has done. In Aurora, Ontario, not far north of Toronto, Trinity Anglican has grown even more rapidly than the burgeoning town and is now planning a major expansion. How has it happened?

When we ask what has brought them to Trinity, Tom and Stacey tell us they are there with their seven-year-old son, Lindsay, because Trinity's ministries meet their needs. Throughout the "905 region," the area around Toronto named after its new telephone area code, other church people give the same answer to the same question.

Tom says he likes the atmosphere of Trinity with its traditional church architecture, its vested clergy and choir, its chandeliers giving off what one poet called "a dim religious light," and wall plaques recalling town pioneers and World War veterans. After a week of high speed on the expressway and high pressure at the office, Tom is ready to recapture the stability he knew as a child, and he finds it at church. He wants it, too, for his son, and Stacey adds she wants Lindsay to learn morals he is not taught at school. "We drive this far because Tom likes the building," she says to explain why they journey past an Anglican church closer to where they live. Then she adds significantly: "Besides, we both like Philip."

"Philip" is the Reverend Canon Philip Poole, incumbent and senior member of Trinity's pastoral team, and Stacey's remark points to a major reason why this cyclical growth church is realizing its potential. Surveys show that most parishioners, especially newer ones, mention Philip as one of their reasons for attending Trinity. Once again, we see how good pastoring can attract people and cause a church to grow.

When Philip arrived in 1986, it was as though his entire career had been designed to prepare him for this opportunity. He had been a camp manager and a school chaplain, as well as assistant curate in a suburban church that was flying high. His first pastorate had been in a commuter community where regular attendance had escalated from 70 to 200, and he had made a point of learning from people what they looked for in a church and what they were finding in his.

He thus arrived at Trinity with a matchless combination of youthful energy and mature knowledge. An organizer, a driver, the kind of human dynamo a cyclical growth church needs, Philip also knew that churches do not grow when they need people. They grow when people believe a church meets their needs.

At Trinity, Sunday attendance has doubled since his arrival, and the projected building expansion will accommodate double the number again. But committed as he is to this $2-million building program, Philip makes people his priority. To help him, he has built a pastoral team of which the Reverend Sharon Melvin is full time, and the Reverends David Flint and Canon Alan Ferguson are part time.

Their team efforts are growing with the church itself. Trinity is now, Philip says, "on the cusp of being a corporate church." Where once he could be at the centre of everything, he now cannot attend every committee and organization meeting, cannot even know everyone who worships at Trinity. The team spreads the load, so that one cleric — and only one — attends each church event.

About 125 members of the congregation meet in small groups, and a team of lay pastoral visitors increases Trinity's personal communication. An innovative dimension of this outreach is a telephone ministry that permits a Sunday service to be transmitted live to the homes of two shut-ins, after which Holy Communion is taken to them that same morning.

But primary as individuals are, the building project is necessary. Trinity has reached the build-or-decline stage of Sunday attendance. Studies show that when a church is regularly filled to 80% capacity, growth slows down and even stops, people seeming to prefer not to be too crowded in the pews. About $500,000 are in the bank, and another $1,800,000 are pledged to expand the old church and provide seating for 500 without losing the traditional church atmosphere that so many value. The project will also include a new parish hall with expanded facilities.

The same is true in another cyclical growth church on the west coast. Vancouver's St. Patrick's is a Roman Catholic church that was once called "the Irish cathedral," from the days when it served a neighbourhood filled by Irish immigrants. Those days have gone now, the descendants of the Irish families having moved elsewhere throughout British Columbia's lower mainland. Even the Italian families that replaced them have moved on, and St. Patrick's might present a sad picture of a once-strong church fallen on hard times. But, no. Its services are well attended and it is raising money for a larger building. With the arrival of Filipinos in the parish, the church is well into its third cycle of growth.

Like Trinity, Aurora, this church has not just watched the newcomers arrive in the neighbourhood. It has gone out to meet them, and its membership has grown because it shows that it cares about them. At its heart was another active priest, the late Reverend Victor Martelino, a Filipino who introduced himself to me in the parking lot with a casual, "Hello. I'm Vic."

Inside, he presides at mass and preaches in impressive English, urging people to follow the Blessed Virgin Mary's example of not clinging to the good things of this world but instead devoting herself to her family. The music is led by an all-female, mostly Filipino choir and organist, and the multicultural congregation joins in heartily.

Before the service, the pastor, the Reverend Don Larson, conducts a Bible study for adults who fill the first two pews and receive a diploma upon completion of the course. When the prayers of the people are offered, the intercessions include prayers for recent converts that "they may feel comfortable in church and join in the work of conversion." These two features reflect Don's background as a Baptist and his zeal as a convert to reach out to others.

The St. Patrick's clergy could be excused if they did not reach out because they have more than enough to occupy them with 1,600 families and singles on their roll and a Sunday attendance of about 2,500. But there is no sign of their concern flagging for those outside the fold. Newcomers are registered each Sunday. A follow-up visit is made by a member of the Legion of Mary. An information package is sent out, plus a welcome letter from Don with an invitation to a coffee hour or some Legion of Mary event.

Don focuses much of his attention on "Catholic affiliates" — people who still see themselves as Roman Catholics but have drifted from the church. He obtains names of parents who register their children at the parochial school but do not come to church, and contacts them. Unbaptized adults are invited into an instructional program that can lead to their initiation as professing Christians.

What will happen when today's Filipino parishioners move on like the Irish and Italians before them? Although Don can expect that other Roman Catholic immigrants will move in, he is obviously not just waiting for that to occur and relying on it to keep the church going. He is making outreach the norm.

So is his denomination as a whole. Don's outreach program is only one example of what the Archdiocese of Vancouver is encouraging churches to attempt. Its chancellor and episcopal vicar for administration, Monsignor Gregory Smith, says that although the archdiocese includes 350,000 baptized Roman Catholics, parish rolls report only 250,000. All the pastors are thus fully supporting the Vatican's call for the year 2000 to be celebrated by a program of world evangelization worthy of the second millennial anniversary of the coming of Jesus Christ. They are not going to let those missing 100,000 lapsed people stay missing. They will seek them out and try to win their hearts.

Cyclical growth is an opportunity, but it is not automatic. It demands what all church growth demands, and its potential is the same where that demand is met.

4. Emerging Growth

Emerging growth occurs when a new church springs up from the grassroots without any historical antecedents.

Canada now contains a number of strong churches that did not exist when the decline of the historic denominations began in the 1960s. While some have evolved from an ecclesiastical ancestry, others have appeared out of the air.

How has it happened? By the application of a simple law of church life: when a human need is not met, a new form of the church will emerge to meet it. It has long been so. Medieval Christianity developed one monastic order after another, each with its own vocation. For the same reason, the Protestant national churches could not contain the Reformation; instead, new sects emerged to meet needs that these churches did not.

One of the country's most dynamic places of worship is an example of this "new/old trend." This extraordinary Winnipeg church grew — really exploded — from a small fellowship of Mennonite Brethren, men and women frustrated in their quest for a contemporary experience in their tradition-based denomination. Unwilling to give up, they started to meet on their own, and by 1992 when their number had grown to 50, they called a pastor, the Reverend Paul Wartman, then serving a Mennonite church in Ontario.

Although neither they nor their new pastor could be precise about what they were seeking, their new church took off, and soon their numbers made a building imperative. But not just any building. It had to be downtown to serve the needs they felt. It had to be different from the church buildings they knew. What could be better than a downtown hotel's night club that had closed because of an economic recession! So they bought it, renovated it, and moved in, the old Bananas Club becoming The Meeting Place, a church that has kept on growing.

At The Meeting Place the style is today's, the content is the Bible's. It is a winning combination.

Before long the church needed two morning services because its 750-seat auditorium was too small to accommodate everybody at once. By 1998, they needed even a third service to accommodate a Sunday total of 2,200. The children's ministry also grew to require a director and a staff to look after the 200 children.

The name The Meeting Place fits. Nothing about it suggests grandeur, inspiration, retreat from the world, or any of the other features of a traditional place of worship: no stained glass, no carved wood, no stone, no brass. It is just a place where people meet to listen and participate. Rows and rows of chairs are banked in concert-hall style to face a platform with musical instruments. A screen is lowered from the ceiling for people to read the words of the songs.

Each Sunday service, planned by a team of the pastors, musicians, and dramatists, revolves around a theme. The planners discuss the sermon Paul will preach, the music to articulate the message, and the dramatization to drive it home. Then they go to work preparing their parts of the service, and meet again on Sunday to put it all together. They meet early, usually at 6:45 a.m., together with audio-visual technicians and the "producer," who acts as something like the master of ceremonies at a high mass. Then the musicians rehearse on their own. So does the drama team. Finally, all re-assemble for prayer, and by 9:30 they are ready for the first service.

The music is entirely contemporary. In fact, The Meeting Place has been called "the rock and roll church." There is excitement in the congregation, nearly all of whom are under 30. People sing up. Some clap their hands and sway.

But there is also substance. The preaching is addressed to real needs. For example, it may focus on people's fears, and the preacher begins by asking what their fears are. Losing their job? their spouse? their health? Then he may review the Bible's message to the fearful, and the brief drama that follows adds impact to the spoken word. Once a sermon on friendship was illustrated by bringing a sports car into the auditorium.

It all lasts one hour. But what an hour!

Yet Sunday worship is not all — 48 small groups, each with eight to 12 members and a facilitator, meet between Sundays. Study, fellowship, and service enable them to experience the personal touch they may not experience at the large Sunday services.

What kind of person is attracted? Twenty-five members are over 60, but the typical age is 30, and a whole year can go by without a funeral, except for the relatives or friends of members. Few come in suits, many in jeans.

Can they keep it all going? Renovating the night club cost $700,000 and the annual budget has grown to over $1-million a year, most of it coming from Sunday offerings. Many members tithe. Twenty per cent of its members have never belonged to a church before. On any given Sunday, 10% of the worshippers are there for the first time. The Meeting Place must be doing a lot of things right.

The message from these churches to any church

❑ **Growth is a potential anywhere.**

Growth churches are found in sociologically diverse communities — urban, suburban, rural, big cities, small towns, among old residents, and among immigrants.

Small churches can achieve growth as well as big ones. Growth does not necessarily mean adding huge numbers. Add 10 new people to a congregation of 20 and you have increased it by 50%.

❑ **We can distinguish four kinds of church growth:**

1. *Expanding growth* occurs when small numbers become bigger as a result of the church's ministry.

2. *Sustaining growth* attracts enough members to equal the inevitable loss that a congregation must suffer each year.

3. When growth in numbers occurs as a result of a demographic change, it may be *cyclical growth*.

4. *Emerging growth* occurs when a new church springs up without any historical antecedents.

A church that wants to grow can begin by analyzing the kinds of growth patterns that are possible for it.

❑ **A dynamic pastor is a huge asset.**

Think of the pastor as the hub of the wheel, other ministers and lay leaders as the spokes, and the congregation as the rim. The wheel cannot function without the hub, spokes, and rim. Everybody has a part to play. But a strong hub holds everything together and gives it force.

Good pastorates are often long pastorates.

❏ **Growth churches are not strait-jacketed by denominational loyalties and traditional denominational ways of doing things.**

1. Growth churches enjoy meaningful relationships beyond their own traditions; for example, receiving information from a multitude of sources.

2. Growth churches do not give priority to persuading newcomers to join the denomination but are content to receive them into their own membership.

3. The worship style in more and more growth churches is an eclectic amalgam from varied sources. They may sing a hymn of Protestant origin at a Roman Catholic mass, or in a Protestant church hear a collect that dates from an early pope's authorship. They may read contemporary choruses from a screen when they are not available in the denomination's hymn book.

4. Some of the pastoral staff of a growth church may have had no training in a denominational seminary. When their particular ministry does not require ordination — music, youth, education, counselling — no one thinks they lack something essential. They may have been trained for their work in the local church itself or in an ecumenical institute.

It is not possible to demand that people toe a denominational party line when, in a free society, they can leave a church as easily as attend it. A denomination may take its stand on doctrine and morality, but the reality is that no one at the local level is bound to accept it.

❑ **A fruitful focus for growth churches is people who have dropped out of churchgoing.**
Why did they leave? Is it because the church appeared to take no interest in them or their needs, or appeared irrelevant or dismissive? If so, there is plenty of opportunity to make up for past negligence or offence.

❑ **Growth churches welcome newcomers.**
Greeters greet them, the pastor publicly welcomes them during the service, they are invited for coffee or lunch afterwards.

Newcomers' names, addresses, and phone numbers are collected. Follow-up phone calls or visits assure them they are welcome. They are given information packages and sometimes small gifts. A newcomers' dinner may follow.

❑ **Holding onto newcomers is as important as welcoming them.**
The service of worship, its music, and its preaching are crucial. Membership in small groups ensures that everybody has the opportunity for fellowship. Groups may concentrate on study, discussion, prayer, service, or practical work. There is enough variety to meet everyone's needs.

❑ **Churches reach a build-or-decline threshold.**
Studies show that when a church is regularly filled to 80% capacity, growth stops because many people prefer to go where they will not be so crowded.

Chapter 3

To grow as it should, a church must first "think growth"

1. "But why should we grow?"

When you walk up Campbell Street in one of Winnipeg's long-established neighbourhoods, you might expect its churches to tell a familiar story of old-time strength giving way to now-time decay. Not so if you go to St. Aidan's Anglican. From the outside it may look like any other half-deserted place of worship, but that appearance is deceiving. St. Aidan's has prayed out its growth potential.

In 1987 when the Reverend Murray Henderson began his ministry there, Sunday attendance was 160, but by 1998 it was averaging 300. The annual budget grew from $350,000 in 1992 to $731,000 just six years later — the largest parish budget in the Diocese of Rupert's Land. The ministry has grown enough to require a priest-associate, the Reverend Merv Lanctot.

"Our growth has not been phenomenal," Murray demurs in his unpretentious rector's study. He points out that the parish list has not lengthened dramatically, but that more people come to church more often. His explanation is simple. "They are coming more because they are finding more."

What that means, however, is not so simple. As a pastor who describes himself as catholic, evangelical, and charismatic, he tries to meet the diversity of needs he finds among his people. They include a number with no inherited commitment to the church and no "brand loyalty" to the denomination. Murray respects how they think. He was one of them.

As a boy, he was introduced to Christianity in two of the city's conservative evangelical churches. But like many of his parishioners, he grew beyond what they had to offer. So he moved, first to the United Church of Canada and later to the Anglican, where he found the spiritual home he had been seeking. At first, Anglicanism appealed because of its sacramental focus and its historical approach to doctrine, but he also discovered it was many-splendoured enough to include the charismatic experience of the Holy Spirit.

As rector, he now presents all facets of that personal evolution in a broad-based church program. Sunday begins with a traditional *Book of Common Prayer* eucharist at which 30 communicants assemble as they might have 30 years ago — or 100. At nine o'clock there is a service for people whose needs are met by worship that includes charismatic features. Then at 11 o'clock, the rector's blending of traditional and contemporary worship styles attracts the largest attendance of the day.

Yet diversity alone does not explain St. Aidan's growth. Other churches, too, have worked at identifying and welcoming newcomers. They have encouraged small groups for Bible study and prayer. They have implemented most of the recommendations learned at growth seminars or in books. But the results have been disappointing. Why?

One answer is that technology does not replace theology. Growth has to factor in one's doctrine of the church for it to occur in one's practice of the church. To grow as it should, a church must first "think growth."

This, as Murray learned, does not come automatically. When Sunday attendance had risen to about 200, he asked a congregational meeting if they were ready for steps that could lead to more growth still. The reaction was neither endorsement nor rejection, but bewilderment. Many parishioners wondered why the rector wanted more growth. Were there not enough people in the pews for strong singing on Sunday mornings? Were there not enough people contributing now to pay the bills? Did St. Aidan's need any more?

Those questions arise when a church thinks only of institutional survival, but Christians committed to the church as God's instrument for the world's salvation have another agenda.

Murray could have challenged his meeting, but prudently he did not. He recognized that people were not ready for the question he had put to them. They needed time to grow together in learning what the church's purpose is. He says now that they had to search out the meaning of the divine commission (Matthew 28:19–20) when at his Ascension, Jesus directed his followers to go into all the world to preach the gospel and make disciples. They had to ask what that meant in Winnipeg now as well as what it meant in Jerusalem then.

People move when impelled by ideas, beliefs, and feelings that have become their own, and St. Aidan's could move only when its people began to "think growth."

But their thinking had to be biblical. Otherwise they could have misunderstood growth as a way of dealing with institutional needs. They had to discover that growth is a force inherent in the church once people ask what it means to be the church as the New Testament understands it. So let us visit two other congregations to see what can happen when people accept the Divine Commission.

2. To close or to grow

In downtown Montreal stand two churches that could have closed years ago. Their residential neighbourhoods were gone. The Anglo population was but a fraction of its former size. What hope was there?

What hope could there be for St. George's Anglican on Montreal's historic Dominion Square, once a prestigious church for prestigious people? Like so many other churches across North America, it went into a slide in the '50's when churchgoing middle-class WASPs (white Anglo-Saxon Protestants) fled to the suburbs. Then the flight of *les anglais* in the face of the threat of Quebec separatism accelerated its decline. St. George's numbers dropped from 377 in 1963 to 146 in 1984.

But in the mid-1980s, a new rector, the Reverend Brett Cane, restored the evangelical focus that had been St. George's long-time emphasis. Along with biblical preaching came services based on the *Book of Common Prayer*. The choir gave up singing to people and led congregational singing instead. A new Sunday school encouraged parents with children. The church began to act as a family. A survey of motives for attending St. George's revealed that the four top reasons were the worship, the clergy, the music, and the friendliness.

St. George's also turned outward to make the best use of its strategic location as a gospel resource. For years it had been closed most of the week for security reasons, but it was reopened for a seven-day-a-week ministry to Montreal. A constant procession of visitors now enters its open doors, joins conducted tours, and listens to its taped inspirational music. Both membership and givings have risen, and there is no more talk of closing the church. A second priest has been added as well as two lay pastoral assistants.

Not far from St. George's on the edge of upscale Westmount, historic St. Stephen's Anglican faces an inspiringly different problem for an inner-city congregation. Where most churches have more plant than people, St. Stephen's has outgrown its building. A majority vote of the membership has already supported staying in this historic location and making the necessary improvements, but a two-thirds majority at a future meeting will be needed for a $1.5-million refurbishment campaign to begin.

Little more than two decades ago, this problem would have seemed fantasy. In 1975 the church had actually been sold to developers, a sad but seemingly inescapable end to a church whose Sunday attendance had dropped to 50. Before the wrecker's ball could swing, however, a new vision of the church appeared. A newly elected Bishop of Montreal, the Right Reverend Reginald Hollis, supported by the neighbourhood as well as the congregation, persuaded the developer to cancel the sale. A new rector, the Reverend Robin Guiness, was then appointed, and a new chapter of parish history began. Average Sunday attendance is now 275. No one now speaks of closure — only of expansion.

Lively worship is one reason for this growth. Associate priest Nick Brotherwood was a professional drummer in a rock band. Music for worship is provided by a group with electronic instruments and audio equipment. The congregation is its own choir, singing words displayed on a large screen at the front.

Priority attention has been given to meeting human needs, bringing people together as a community, and motivating them to serve Christ in the world. At the back of the building, where pews once stood, is a space for people to gather before and after services for coffee and conversation. Coming from all over the west end of the island of Montreal, they make the most of Sunday as their only time for meeting each other. Eating together is a regular feature of their church life. Sandra Guiness, the rector's wife, not only organizes the Sunday coffees but also hosts six welcome dinners a year in her home for newcomers. The old rectory, next door to the church hall, is to be transformed into offices and a hospitality centre, so that the St. Stephen's ministry can be expanded.

In its present state of repair, the building would not win a prize, but in its present condition as a human community, the church might — and mostly because clergy and people have taken the divine commission seriously.

That this kind of activity can be undertaken so effectively is all the more impressive because St. Stephen's suffers a 20% membership turnover each year — an almost complete change every five years. That might discourage a church with less of a "mission mentality," but not this one. To maintain its vitality, it has developed programs designed to incorporate newcomers rapidly, and to show them how they can be part of a fellowship that is as welcoming as it is changing.

We have visited three growth churches that could have declined or even closed. We have seen what a difference comes from gaining a sense of mission. It is time for us to reflect on the source of that mission.

3. The God of Growth

Christian action is based on theology. An ideology is a scheme of ideas at the base of some political or economic theory or system. It may be good ideology and serve as the motivation and guide for worthwhile actions. However, it only becomes theology when it is transformed by God's revelation in Jesus Christ. The church always acts theologically. Church growth only serves Christ when it rises up from theological ground.

The theological imperative for church growth lies in what Christianity believes about God himself. God is a God of growth, and a church professing to witness to God must seek to grow.

God the Creator

To believe in creation means to believe that nature cannot explain itself: nature points beyond itself for explanation. Creation was not a single event that occurred billions of years ago. Nor is it a phenomenon that only astronomers and geologists can understand. We watch it occur before our own eyes.

For 25 years I cultivated a vegetable garden on the one patch of arable soil on our two acres of the Precambrian Shield. I did not do it to save money, since it was cheaper to buy vegetables at the store. The reason was theological. Nowhere else did I marvel at the mystery of creation more than in that garden. Plants pushed their tiny but determined heads up through soil into which they had been placed as "eyed" pieces of potato or as hard lifeless-looking seeds. To see it happen was like being present at the first morning of creation, like being witness to a wondrous act that could be described but not explained. This miraculous happening pointed beyond itself to the One who was making it happen. My garden was growing because the God of growth, the Creator, willed the world to be a place of growth.

Early one morning, this message came more dramatically still. As I hoed my potatoes, my silent solitude was interrupted by what sounded like distant trumpet blasts. They were the loud honks of Canada geese returning north from their winter retreat. Minutes later, they flew overhead in a majestic V formation, and reminded me of something about being human. The geese, the potatoes, and I were all creatures, all sharing the same creation, all joined together in one ecological harmony, receiving life from the same God and sharing it as God's creatures. To live is both to grow and to make growth.

In the Bible, the faithfulness of God the Creator is witnessed age after age, in seedtime and harvest, in every bird that flies, in every human that is born. To believe in the God of the Bible is to affirm life, to join God in the joyous, dynamic experience he enables the humblest creature to share.

The primary value expressed in the Bible is not faith, hope, or love, but life. The Bible begins with the story of life's beginning and ends with a picture of life's renewal. "Choose life" was the cry that rallied Israel, and the good news of the risen Christ was the new life that empowered the apostolic church and sent it forth to grow and grow.

To witness to this, God demands that a church be committed to growth. Like the Bible, it must find the meaning of God in pictures of life as a moving, growing mystery, such as these four lines describe:

The way of an eagle in the sky,
the way of a serpent on a rock,
the way of ship on the high seas,
the way of a man with a maiden. *(Proverbs 30:19)*

A church is a lively fellowship when its people believe in a God of life. It is a Nietzschean sepulchre, a morgue, a death house when it does not point beyond itself to the Creator.

In the Old Testament, God's promise to Abraham as father of the nation of Israel was that his descendants should multiply as the stars of the heaven (Genesis 15:5). Each life born into that nation was welcomed as a gift from God; each convert from the Gentiles was baptized in living water as a sign of being "born again" to be one of God's own people. The story of Israel was a testimony to the God of growth.

Consequently, in scripture there is none of the inhibition about discussing numbers that we find in some churches. The Bible reports feeding 5,000 and converting 3,000. It counts 12 apostles and 120 witnesses to our Lord's Ascension. St. Paul, too, takes obvious satisfaction in his reports of growth in newly founded churches. Numbers are not the whole story, not even the main part of it, but they are not omitted from the telling. Churches of our own day need have no shame in counting numbers.

Sceptics about the importance of church growth do not make a strong case when they assert that spiritual growth matters more than numerical increase. God is not honoured by a crowded church where there is minimal faith, hope, and love, but neither is he honoured in a nearly empty one that is bereft of them. The reluctance of some Christians to acknowledge the importance of numbers is based on a foundation of sand. To give numbers their due place is part of witnessing to God as Creator, to the God of growth.

For almost two millennia, Christianity has grown because it has taken that witness seriously. From the first congregation gathered at Pentecost in Jerusalem until now, the number of believers has multiplied from 120 to almost two billion. There has been nothing in history to equal it, the total Christian population of the world exceeding that of any faith or country. It is the greatest growth story the world has ever known, an inspiring testimony to what can happen when churches take God the Creator seriously.

The Saviour

The story of Jesus, the incarnate son of God, reminds us that to be human is to grow. As a quarter-of-an-inch-long embryo he began his life in the womb of Mary. Soon tissues from her body wrapped themselves around that embryo to provide it with oxygen, water, and food through an umbilical cord that also carried away waste. By the end of eight weeks a human head and body, with all their organs, was growing. Seven months later, in a manger behind an inn at the small town of Bethlehem, the baby's head pushed out of Mary's womb. And then the child "grew in stature": baby, child, teenager. Two hundred years later, Irenaeus, a bishop in Lyons, explained our salvation in terms of the incarnate son of God proceeding through every age and stage from infancy to maturity. To save us all, baby or senior citizen, he grew from the time he lay in a cradle until the day he lay in a tomb.

To speak of the church now as the body of Christ is to speak of growth as part of the church's being. The church is the body of the risen and living Christ, and its growth proclaims that Christ is alive and well and working in his churches.

In his teaching, Jesus used images of growth to illustrate his message of the new life. Believers should be as prolific as mustard seed. As a tree was known by the fruit it grew, the faith of his followers would be known by their lives. In deed as well as in word, Jesus' message was always about this life of growth. He made the lame to walk, the deaf to hear, the blind to see, the dead to rise. Thousands were fed from a few loaves and fishes. Water was changed into wine to signify the new life Jesus was offering to men and women. He broke bread and blessed it, then took a cup of wine and gave thanks, and both these elements testify to the life that believers share.

With this message of growth to guide them, the churches of the apostolic age grew so dynamically that around the year A.D. 400, Augustine of Hippo would write that, marvellous as the miracles of Jesus had been, greater still was the miracle of the church's growth. There had been nothing like it before. There has not been since.

For two millennia, the church has grown as no other society, sacred or secular, ever has. It is older than any nation. It has outlived every empire. Its growth will never stop until at last even the gates of hell will open before it.

The Sanctifier

Although the food that makes growth possible comes from outside a body, growth occurs within it. So with the new life the gospel offers. It results from a power growing within us. This is the Holy Spirit, the presence of God affirmed and witnessed in baptism as a new birth, the presence that brings believers to life, empowering them to grow and to give growth.

In the words of the Nicene creed, the Spirit is "the Lord and Giver of life." In the New Testament, we are taught to picture the Spirit as air or fire or water, three of the four elements that ancient culture taught were the essence of reality.

Although humans can live without food for days, we cannot live without air for more than minutes. Our lives thus depend upon an invisible element. It is a challenge for us now to recognize the consequences if air pollution continues to grow worse, so that the air is no longer a giver of life. It is no less a challenge to recognize that the invisible Spirit of God is just as essential for life.

The earth's surface is more than half covered with water, and water is the principal component of our bodies. Plants cannot grow without it. We drink it. We wash in it. We cook with it. One of the crises we may face in the twenty-first century is a shortage of water. We cannot live without it. Similarly, we cannot live without the Spirit. Baptism in water witnesses to the Spirit as life giver.

Fire, too, is essential for life. There would be no life without the fire of the sun to provide both warmth and light. A fetus is given warmth in the womb and a newborn is protected from the cold by being wrapped in a blanket. We speak of acceptance, friendship, and belonging as providing warmth and of their absence as cold. Like the sun, the Spirit is our source of warmth and light and life.

The apostolic church grew because of the Spirit's presence. Wherever the Spirit was, the good news of the new life was preached and the church grew. In our times, too, the Spirit's presence manifests in all the ministries that cause a church to grow.

Of course, it would be a mistake to infer that the Spirit is absent when a church does not grow. It is God who sets the schedule for growth. But we may legitimately ask whether the Spirit is present in a church where there is no desire for growth. The church of the New Testament was too filled with the Spirit even to think that way. As "the fellowhip of the Holy Spirit," it had to think growth.

Being and Becoming

We are left with a question: if God so clearly intends that the church should grow, why do some churches place growth so low on their agenda?

The answer is the theological mistake of thinking about the church as *being* instead of *becoming*. The Bible affirms that God is always *becoming*. It devotes no attention to questions about God's existence. Instead it always affirms God's work in the world.

A *being* church possesses an "establish-mentality"; a *becoming* church is driven by a "mission-mentality."

We can easily confuse the church with structures believed to make up its *being*. We do this when we identify the church with an established order that includes the scriptures, creeds, sacraments, and ministries. The church, of course, must have structure. But the church is called not merely to conserve scripture, creeds, and the rest. It is called to become more — to grow into the Kingdom of God. A church that is *becoming* possesses scriptures, creeds, sacraments, and ministries, but it sees them as instruments to serve its calling as a church. As the servant of the God of *becoming*, it is the witness to the God who forgives sins, heals sicknesses, reconciles alienations, rights wrongs. It expresses itself in growth because salvation is its priority. It grows because it is not content just to be. It always seeks to become.

That is the Bible's way. All its statements about God are about God in relationship to people and the world. About God on his own, the Bible is silent. It tells us that God wants men and women to become the truly human beings that God intends them to be: an insecure shepherd like Moses becomes a liberator, a rural worker like Amos becomes a prophet, a whore like Mary Magdalene becomes a saint, a persecutor like Paul becomes an apostle, handfuls of unnamed men and women become churches.

The difference between *being* and *becoming* is not academic but decisive. To seek growth or to ignore it is a theological decision.

The message of churches that "think growth"

❏ **Growth occurs when a church recognizes that growth is a basic theological principle.**

Growth is not an addendum. God the Creator, God the Saviour, God the Sanctifier is the God of Growth.

❏ **The divine commission commands growth.**

"Go forth and make all nations my disciples; baptize people everywhere in the name of the Father and the Son and the Holy Spirit, and teach them to observe all that I have commanded you. And be assured, I am with you always, to the end of time." *(Matthew 28: 19–20)*

❏ **Churches need never be ashamed of counting numbers.**

The Bible is full of number counts. St. Paul was proud of his churches' growth in numbers. The church's history is the world's most phenomenal growth story. Although a full church may not be a guarantee of sanctity and spiritual commitment, neither is a nearly empty one.

Chapter 4

Growth churches have not followed a formula, but they have evolved a pattern

Although there is no formula that will guarantee growth, churches that grow show common patterns. Other churches that decide to grow can follow the patterns. There is no need to reinvent the wheel.

To identify patterns of growth and draw conclusions from them may seem inhibiting to those who think that spirituality demands spontaneity. But the biblical way is an orderly way. The Bible begins with a description of the order of creation; the gospels show that Jesus' ministry followed a plan, that the apostolic churches were taught to do everything "decently and in good order."

The work of God does not exclude organization. No plant that shoots up from the ground, no body that develops to maturity does so by accident. Each follows a design inherent within it from the beginning. So do growth churches.

Yes, the spontaneous and the miraculous are also part of the church's life and work. Nonetheless, the Bible shows that God works in patterns alongside those unpredictable, inexplicable miracles he performs. Miracles are not more divine than the order of the seasons by which nature is governed. In his sixteenth-century classic, *The Laws of Ecclesiastical Polity*, Richard Hooker asserted that God not only established laws for the world and humanity, but also governed even himself by his own law. This law he followed in the creation and in the new creation he revealed in Jesus Christ.

It is certainly possible for a church to follow a pattern and yet not grow, just as it is possible for a church to ignore patterns and grow anyway; the Spirit blows where the Spirit wills. However, the churches we are visiting manifest the same features and evidence common patterns, whether they are large or small, urban or rural, WASP or ethnic, this denomination or that.

This pattern is a pentagon, a pattern with five sides:

Priorization of growth
Responsiveness to people's needs
Quality
Creativity
Personal touch

Priorization of Growth

Instead of treating growth as an ancillary interest, growth churches understand that it is intrinsic to the body of Christ. They know that an organism cannot stay alive without growth. Growth is always at the top of the agenda, right up there with the other essentials. Let us therefore visit a few churches to see what giving growth priority means in action as well as words.

Deer Park United on the edge of Calgary became what it is through cyclical growth, but to sustain growth it has established a Membership and Growth Committee in its governance structure alongside the committees most churches have. One of the church's two clergy, the Reverend Jennifer Ferguson, is the staff member of this committee, helping it to be proactive with fresh ideas. Her husband and co-minister, the Reverend John Pentland, respects numbers enough to know exactly how many people they serve: 1,501.

At each of the two Sunday services, a "Friendship Folder" is passed along the pews. A white plastic, hardcover binder, it contains a card for newcomers to complete with their names, addresses, and telephone numbers. In the week following, a member of the Membership and Growth Committee telephones the newcomer with a message of welcome and to obtain relevant information.

But the committee does not wait for people to show up on their own. It also receives the names of persons who arrange weddings and baptisms at the church and invites them to a get-to-know-you barbecue. At the last barbeque, 75 showed up. It also distributes information and invitation literature to make sure the church's neighbours know it is there and is open for them. The committee concerns itself with something routine and unexciting but unconditionally imperative: keeping the church's membership records up to date.

Jennifer and John also make sure their church is not alienating to seekers. Many of the newcomers have had no Christian education at all. The Bible may be foreign literature to some of them, and they might leave a church service feeling they had been visiting a strange land. Outreach means addressing people where they are. So, for 10 months in 1997 and 1998, Jennifer and John replaced the regular lectionary in order to take people through the Bible from Genesis to Revelation. Sermons, music, dramatizations, and children's program were coordinated to provide worshippers with a systematic introduction to the Bible.

What difference are these and other efforts making? Attendance at Sunday worship has grown to 500 at two services through most of the year. Of that total, 5% are new to Christianity and 40% started at Deer Park within the previous five years. Something is happening.

But to make sure it stays happening, John and Jennifer are leading their church in an envisioning program to get a clear picture of the church they would like to be in the future and to decide how they can make the picture become real. They have taken a Spiritual Gifts Inventory, so that people can see what they have to offer each other and what they can receive. Deer Park United assumes that if their church has a common goal, it will continue to advance.

The pattern that Deer Park is following can be duplicated by others ready to search for growth and make it a prominent, regular feature of their church life.

Over the mountains in Vancouver's Anglican Church of the Good Shepherd, we find yet another congregation committed to mission. On its pastoral staff alongside two clergy — the Reverend Stephen Leung, rector, and the Reverend Philip Der, assistant curate — is a full-time woman evangelist, Catherine Mok. Her ministry includes expanding outreach to Chinese women in a program of adult education, Bible study, and house groups as well as regular pastoral care.

Catherine's work is an indication of the way Good Shepherd unites outreach and pastoral care. Founded in 1903 to pastor the city's Chinese immigrants, the church still provides spiritual fellowship for Vancouver's increasing Chinese population, and it is growing with its community. Once a subsidized mission, it is now a self-supporting parish of the Diocese of New Westminster with an annual budget of $250,000.

Stephen points out that membership would be larger, but Good Shepherd planted another Chinese Anglican church in nearby Richmond and gave up 100 families to the new church. Within a year, not only did the new church double in size, but Good Shepherd replaced its "departures" by as many newcomers. This was the second new church Good Shepherd had founded, and all are still growing.

The ministry to youth grips you when you attend the nine o'clock eucharist at Good Shepherd. In how many other Anglican churches can you find a congregation where almost everyone is under age 30? The service is designed for young people. A table beneath the chancel steps takes the place of the more distant altar. A youth group supplies the music, the songs are sung from words projected on a screen, and the singing is punctuated by evangelical messages from a young woman in T-shirt and jeans. Everyone is dressed down except the priest presiding over the Holy Mysteries in a white alb. The worship is unpretentiously reverent, but when the Peace is exchanged, the worshippers are out in the aisle greeting one another, hugging and smiling with the joy of meeting after a week apart.

At the service later in the morning, the ethos is traditional and formal as befits the congregation of people from a different generation and culture. But the nine o'clock service shows that Good Shepherd sets a high priority on service for youth.

That readiness to serve people shows us the next feature in the pentagon pattern that growth churches follow.

Responsiveness to People's Needs

Growth churches shape their programs in response to needs people are feeling, rather than expecting people to accept a program that they lay on. Church life is more a "bottom-up" development than a "top-down" proclamation. Clergy and lay leaders carry on continual dialogue with people to ensure that real needs are identified and met.

We have already visited Montreal's People's Church, where most church meetings are held on the same night, so that entire families can attend together, a "must" when they are scattered all over the island of Montreal. Let us now visit a Roman Catholic church just west of Toronto that, according to Cardinal Archbishop Aloysius Ambrozic, is "bursting at the seams." Why? This Mississauga church is crowded because its pastor cares so much about people that he designs ministries to meet their needs.

Tradition is strong at St. John of the Cross, but so is contemporaneity. The church's leaders are responding to people as they are and not just as they used to be. The neighbourhood looks like any of the "bedroom" communities that have proliferated in the region called the GTA (Greater Toronto Area) that now has a population larger than seven of Canada's provinces. The scene is familiar: two or more cars parked in the driveways of family homes, each with two bathrooms, many with two mortgages.

But this neighbourhood also demonstrates social change.

Not very long ago, the "burbs" were all WASP, and more recently arrived immigrants were concentrated in the older inner city. But now the second generation of immigrant families is affluent enough to move out and move up. This new prosperity has brought problems as well as comforts, and pastoral challenges to churches. Where once it could be assumed that people who wanted to retain their old-country lifestyle also wanted to enjoy an old-country type of church, the second- and third-generation people now live new-style all week. An otherwise traditional church needs to offer programs and ministries to meet their needs.

At St. John of the Cross, therefore, the Reverend Marcel Dubé includes a support group for divorcees. Without diluting the Roman Catholic Church's firm teaching against divorce, this group pastors people who are trying to put their lives back together. They need the church as a caring community and can better accept being judged if they know they are also loved.

In the vestibule of the church office, you read this message:

Awake at dawn with a winged heart
for another day of loving.

It may seem unusual to encounter a quotation from Kahlil Gibran in a Roman Catholic church. But this church practises Justin

Martyr's second-century counsel, "Take truth where you find it," and makes responding to needs its priority.

When visitors enter the church, they find that although it has everything a Roman Catholic place of worship normally has, it has them with a difference. The altar displays a flame motif symbolizing St. John carrying a flame up to the cross on a hill surrounded by flames. Behind the altar is the president's chair, and on either side of it are two lecterns. As well as an organ, there is a Yamaha keyboard, and there are folding chairs for the two choirs. This is a church for the late twentieth century.

Here the program is shaped to meet the needs of people who have strayed from the church as well as those who have remained faithful. RCIA (Rite of Christian Initiation of Adults) is a regular part of parish life; 25 adults were received at Easter 1997, about half by baptism. When parents request baptism for their children, they are first interviewed by Father Bob Boley or Deacon Peter McBride. There is liaison with the local Roman Catholic schools to learn which families are not on the church rolls and to make contact.

St. John of the Cross keeps four clergy busy every day, and the staff includes two secretaries, a custodian, a housekeeper, and a music director. But other laity also share in 47 ministries. A St. Vincent De Paul program serves people on low incomes. A liturgy committee shapes worship that responds to needs and coordinates the large number of laity involved in the services as lectors, ushers, and acolytes. The New Beginnings group pastors people who have been separated, divorced, or widowed. Eighty people are in Bible study groups that meet in homes. Once a year, a Commitment Sunday gives people a chance to choose the kind of church work they want to do.

With all these ministries at work, the parish rolls have almost doubled — 2,300 families in 1987, and 4,300 in 1997. That this expansion has also changed the face of the church from white to multi-ethnic has not made for division. Marcel comments that there is "a good spirit" among his people. Everyone is content that English should be the language of the mass, but there is a Caribbean choir at the Saturday service, and an East Indian mass on Sunday.

With this kind of growth, accommodation is under pressure on regular Sundays and all but impossible at great festivals. So a larger church building has been planned and a building fund begun. The new facilities will include an expanded worship centre, increased meeting space, more washrooms, and a much larger foyer to be what the pastor calls "a place to stop and talk." The massive size and vaulted roofs of churches used to make a triumphalist statement. The new St. John of the Cross will be a "people place."

Responsiveness, however, need not reduce a church to a kind of humanism with a religious face. It involves also a conscious responsiveness to God's calling and guiding his churches, a responsiveness in which prayer is prominent. At Regina's Celebration Lutheran, which we have already visited, Dan Sattelmaier testifies to his sensing "a supernatural power at work." In downtown Calgary we will find a church that was resurrected when it responded to what may have been a unique message from God.

At the base of Calgary's Tower, the prairies' tallest structure, is a vast complex of shops, boutiques, restaurants, and services in the kind of indoor mall found all over North America and increasingly in Europe. But this may be the only one that contains a church — the church meets in a cinema!

The Jubilee Christian Centre rose phoenix-like from the ashes of a previous congregation that had suffered a drop in numbers from 3,000 to 350 and was in financial crisis. The entire enterprise could have disappeared but for the confidence of one man. Phil Nordin's whole career had been preparing him for the challenge. As a youth he had done evangelistic work with his sister and her husband. Later he and his wife had ministered to street people and then started churches in three British Columbia cities. He and the remaining congregation of Jubilee had to sell their building to pay down their debt. Dissolving the congregation might have been the next step, but something else happened.

According to Phil, seated in his well-equipped Tower office, it was prayer. Shortly after he took over, two visiting Ugandan Christians arrived and told him that God had sent them to help him save the church.

He might have sent them away, but he was intrigued and he wondered what their strategy — or magic — might be. What a shock! It was not something new and wonderful at all; it was something as old and familiar as an all-night prayer vigil. They wanted to start that very night by calling together all the church members who could come and pray from midnight till six in the morning.

Phil rounded up some of his key people and the vigil was held that same night, and it was repeated every night for three weeks, when these strangers left as suddenly as they had arrived. Who could have planned an event like that? It was like a story from the Acts of the Apostles.

Although the two men disappeared, they left a legacy behind. The church is still holding a prayer vigil every Friday evening from eight p.m. until ten p.m. Phil is convinced it is the soil from which his church has grown, the soil of responding to God.

The response began with acts to restore confidence in the church's leadership, such as making full financial disclosure to the members, and holding a service of reconciliation with the former pastor instead of imputing blame for what had happened. Next, since the congregation had nowhere to hang their hats, they rented office space at the bargain-basement rate of $2 per square foot in Calgary's then-depressed downtown. Soon they were able to rent a cinema in the Tower as a place for Sunday worship. The chain that owned it was glad to receive some extra revenue. Although it might have seemed an unsuitable place to worship God, the gospel began in a stable, and the congregation showed itself ready for this new venue.

It was not easy for the church's leadership. After the Sunday 10 a.m. service, all the church equipment had to be cleared out for the two p.m. movie matinee. When that was over, the place had to be set up again for church again at 4:30. It was a demanding schedule, but it worked. Morning attendance rose to about 500. Before long the services were drawing more than the movies, and the cinema chain was happy to transfer its lease for the premises to the church. Phil and his people had a spiritual home again.

Jubilee presents the gospel in ways every bit as interesting as the movies. Music in today's tempo is provided by electronic instruments and drums. It is loud when everyone is clapping and singing along. The preaching is biblically based, but it deals with contemporary issues like abortion, sex education, and healing. The average age of worshippers is 35. A "Super Church" draws 90 children to their own Sunday service in an adjacent auditorium, a former second cinema. A Youth Department now involves up to 80 young people in a ministry that includes not only their own programs but missionary service as far-away as Argentina. The church staff includes a pastoral counsellor, administrative personnel, and five elders who visit the sick. The church pays the parking charge for worshippers who leave their cars at the Tower's Inpark facility — a welcome "perk" for people who drive long distances.

People in a church like this are inspired to help others. Jubilee is building an orphanage in Puebla, Mexico, to house 75 homeless children. To be made of plastic components in Canada at a cost of $200,000, this structure is the result of Phil's visiting this city of three million, being stirred by the needs he saw, linking up with a Puebla pastor, and then arranging for six other Jubilee people to go there and catch the vision of what could be done.

St. John of the Cross, Mississauga, and Jubilee Christian Centre, Calgary, are growing partly because they take the trouble to learn what people's real needs are and respond directly to them. But a church doesn't have to be big, play drums, or meet in a cinema to respond to people's needs, as our next visit to a rural Ontario community shows.

Quality

When an organization is staffed by volunteers and financed by voluntary contributions, it is tempting to take a "second best will do" attitude—but that is a mistake growth churches do not make. They know that the quality of their facilities, program, and personnel are part of their appeal. More profoundly, they believe that a worthy offering to God, whose Son gave his all, demands nothing less than the best. What is good enough for a church has to be good enough for the Lord. It must be the best a church can offer.

Large or small, urban or rural, high income or average, growth churches show they care about the quality of their ministry. Facilities may be sophisticated or simple, but they reflect the believers' commitment by being tidy, clean, and spacious. Music is as inspiring as the resources available can make it. Preaching is relevant to people's needs. Sunday school is imaginative and makes the best quality use possible of human, print, video, and other resources. Clergy and lay leaders accept the demand that doing the Lord's work requires apostolic commitment. That may be as simple as making sure vestments are clean and pressed, or as vital as devoting ample time to sermon preparation. When newcomers leave a growth church, they feel it has been a privilege to worship there, a privilege they want to enjoy again.

Quality is not the special preserve of large city churches strong in resources. So let us visit a small country church in southern Ontario's lake country, northeast of Toronto, one whose structure was so unsound that it was in danger of being condemned by municipal authorities and closed by church officials. But St. John's Anglican Church, Harwood, is now open 25 weeks a year to serve a seasonal community of holiday-makers.

The transformation began with people recognizing that if they loved this place with all their hearts, they would make it go with all their might. One of them was the Honourable Pauline Browes, a former Canadian cabinet minister, who committed her legendary personal energy to making this church a vibrant fellowship again. With others of a like mind, she spearheaded a drive to convince church authorities that St. John's could be viable.

Knowing that people want a lift when they come to church, her team arranged some Sunday programs to raise people's spirits and send them away saying, "Lord, it has been good to be here." During the holiday season, they included five theme services in which everything would be focused on a designated message.

On Canada Day the lawn was covered with national flags and festooned with umbrellas, the children all received small flags, the music included "O Canada," the prayers included petitions for the country, and afterwards everyone enjoyed a cake decorated with a national flag.

On Hat Day, when everyone wore favourite hats — old straw hats, baseball hats, Tilley hats, Shakespearean hats — the rector, the Reverend John Saynor, donned a stetson when he gave the blessing. Afterwards, everyone went outside to enjoy candy floss on the lawn.

On Country and Western Day, everyone wore cowboy costume; prize-winning horses were brought for display; and the children were given pony rides and hot dogs after Sunday school. Crazy? Irreverent? Everyone went home convinced St. John's was a good place to be on Sunday morning.

On Youth Day, 23 graduates of the Vacation Bible School received certificates, and boys and girls provided the readings and music at the service. Parents and grandparents jammed the church.

A church to be closed because nobody came thus stayed open with an average Sunday attendance of 53. The congregation also raised enough money to repair the building and to pay their realtor for the five months the church is open.

What had made the difference between life and death, growth and inertia? First-class effort. First-class enthusiasm. First-class creativity. First-class everything. The result: a first-class church.

Now, unlike many rural churches, St. John's is fully self-supporting financially and is expanding its ministry. John Saynor has brought in some experts to launch a summer day-camp program. He has introduced services on Christmas Eve and at Easter that are crowded out, and he has even added a four o'clock service on summer Sundays for those who love the incomparably beautiful Anglican evensong.

Doing everything in a quality way is essential for growth. And while it is obvious in large churches like Winnipeg's The Meeting Place or Regina's Celebration Lutheran, it is equally obvious in small churches like St. John's Harwood and Knox Church, Port Carling. In fact, it is the reason why a small church like Coldstream United Baptist has grown so dramatically. What it demands is not wealth but dedication. And some creativity.

Creativity

Although membership in the United Church of Canada has been falling, many of its congregations are growing. St. David's, Calgary, whose Sunday attendance of 600 at two services makes it the third-largest in the denomination, not only thinks growth but does what it takes to create it.

One such thing was calling the Reverend Don Wright to leave a Canadian Armed Forces chaplaincy and devote a few years to a church open to his creative approach. When I visited him, Don fired ideas at machine-gun speed. Some ideas came from steady reading — a book a week — on what is shaping our culture. Other ideas were his own, like the Church Triad Planning System he used to restructure life at St. David's. The Triad program divided the church year into three parts, each focused on one facet of the church's life: spirituality (January through April), finances (May through August), and leadership (September through December).

Don was convinced that growth churches must take risks and do things differently; so at St. David's summer became the time for budget-planning and pledge-soliciting. "When everyone else is shutting down," he said, "we're cranking up." It makes sense, he insisted, because people have paid their income tax and perhaps have some surplus cash from a rebate. "They are sitting around waiting for you to ask them for money!"

Ask them this church did, starting at the end of May with a talent auction at which adults and children offer services for sale with the proceeds going to the church. One child raised $150 with an offer to write a letter once a month to someone who was lonely. Over the summer, income earners were asked to pledge the equivalent of an hour's income as their Sunday offering. A person working a 40-hour week for an annual salary of $35,000 would thus pledge $16.82 a week, or $870.64 a year. There are three special appeals a year — at Easter, Thanksgiving, and Christmas — and donors are thanked at three stewardship dinners.

At the end of each trimester of the Triad year, a congregational meeting planned the transition to the next phase of church life. Current members brought newcomers to this event that sometimes drew 1,000 people. At the September meeting, leadership was the topic. Job descriptions of volunteer positions were published in a booklet, so that people could choose one that suited their time and talent. Don cautioned people to consider their own energy level because burn-out could be a major reason for lay leadership faltering. The autumn months were devoted to recruiting, training, and integrating leaders.

From January through April, the focus was on spirituality, that is, growing as a Christian person. A church that aims only at increasing numbers, Don insisted, will fail because people have another priority — the quality of their lives. The church that improves the quality of their lives holds value for them.

Don's sermons during these months focused on the quality of life. His subjects ranged far and wide: the parable of the vineyard workers (the last shall be first and the first last — the most for the least), a discussion of a current best seller, the Jesus Seminar's attempt to describe what kind of human being Jesus actually was.

Music in worship was also carefully planned. The service began with a children's hymn before the boys and girls went to classes. St. David's was also preparing its own hymn book. The Genesis People, 120 strong, occasionally sang and once presented *Godspell*. Five special music events were advertised in a newsletter, along with 12 vocal and instrumental opportunities for adults and children.

To keep this powerhouse of a church generating more power required a full-time staff of eight, plus hundreds of volunteers. The congregation also issued its own Statement of Faith, Purpose, and Vision. Nothing in it was at variance with the denomination, but it clarifies St. David's own directions — a further sign of the church's creativity.*

We have now constructed four sides of the pentagon. The figure is not complete until we add the personal touch, without which no church is true to its calling.

* The minister at St. David's now is Dr. Ralph Spencer.

The Personal Touch

Few churches omit the personal touch from their life. Greeters welcome people as they arrive, clergy shake hands as people leave, members of large congregations form small groups, the sick and the troubled are offered pastoral care. But the Muskoka Christian Fellowship puts the personal touch at the centre. It is a community made up of many cells.

It began not as a congregation that later divided into groups, but as groups that formed a congregation. In the town of Bracebridge, Ontario, with its 12 places of Christian worship, David and Linette Boyes were looking for one that was more oriented to youth and mission. After much soul searching, reflection, and study, they conceived the idea of small group fellowships being like the cells of a body. A series of meetings with others in town resulted in a decision to form the kind of cell-based church some of them had read about but none had ever experienced. About 20 agreed to try it for six weeks and then to review the situation and decide whether to carry on or close down.

In a rented conference room at the Riverside Inn on the banks of the picturesque Muskoka River, they met on a Sunday in 1994. After an opening period of worship, they divided into two cells. Out of this evolved their meeting as cells in people's homes and coming together every other Sunday as a fellowship. The number of cells grew, and so did attendance at the bi-weekly fellowship services.

Membership in a cell is limited to 12 to 15, a cell dividing when that number is reached. Each cell has two leaders who maintain a quasi-pastoral relationship with the members. David

Boyes has gradually assumed a ministry as pastor to these leaders and to the fellowship as a whole.

At the cell meetings, the priority is fellowship and sharing with one another both blessings and cares. Open group confessions are not practised, but cell members have the option to confide in the cell leader if they feel the need. Worship at a cell meeting includes singing, testifying, Bible study, and mission. Each cell develops a way of serving either the community or one another, such as visiting seniors' homes, helping single mothers, or joining in an event like the town's annual March for Jesus.

The fellowship brings all the cells together every other Sunday. On the intervening Sunday, members are urged to render some practical service such as visiting shut-ins or relatives, inviting neighbours in for lunch, or doing some other good deed.

At the bi-weekly service in the Riverside Hotel, most of the worshippers are young. The music is led by a song leader who also plays a guitar and is assisted by a drummer. People sing with enthusiasm, and some elevate their hands to show praise. David stands behind a lectern that bears a coloured cross and crown — the only obvious liturgical symbol.

The most striking difference from mainline Protestant worship comes at the prayer time when worshippers are invited to make requests. One man proudly announces his wife has just learned she is pregnant. A woman tells of her daughter's basement being flooded. Another shares the grim news that her adopted child has been diagnosed with a serious syndrome. Still another reports that her nephew has suffered a critical eye injury. Prayer is requested also for fellowship members away at a women's retreat, and for the coming garage sale sponsored by the youth ministry. This is worship in which people share personal concerns and reach out to each other and the world in prayer.

The Muskoka Christian Fellowship has grown so much since 1994 that it has planted another fellowship in nearby Parry Sound and formed a cell group in Huntsville, not far away. Already there are enough members and revenue to maintain the work without subsidy from a denomination, to pay David for his full-time ministry and to appoint a pastor for the Parry Sound church. With characteristic enthusiasm, David has drafted plans to start other fellowships throughout Ontario.

The Muskoka Christian Fellowship shows the power that can be generated when people experience what the New Testament means when it describes the church as the fellowship of the Holy Spirit.

That small groups are not the only way to provide personal fellowship is shown in the renewal of a multipoint Anglican parish in rural New Brunswick. At one of its churches, Holy Trinity, Hartland, on the banks of the historic St. John River, the Reverend Peter Gillies boasts the fastest-growing parish in the country in percentage terms.

In communities like Hartland, most people know each other well, but Peter stresses the personal by involving so many people in the services that they are a community experience. Attendance has grown since 1995 from an average of seven to twenty. Sunday worship is now at the difficult hour of one o'clock, and Peter hopes to encourage younger families to attend by shifting the service to the morning. With the accent on the personal more than the professional, he will use the services of qualified lay readers.

He has already raised the number of lay readers and servers as part of his plan to encourage people of all ages to get involved. Once a month, he hands over the entire service to lay people while he sits in the pew with his family.

Sometimes all the people of his multipoint parish meet in one of the churches for Sunday worship followed by a meal. The services suit the rural community.

One Rogation Sunday, for example, when Anglicans pray for God's blessing on the seed to be sown in the ground, he united all his congregations into one eucharist — at a farm instead of a church, with a board laid across two bales of hay to form the altar.

The more we find our lives taken over by technology, the more we want them to retain a personal dimension. Churches can use every high-tech instrument there is, but they grow most when they recognize that personal caring is what matters.

Near the populous commuter community of Markham, Ontario, one of Canada's most distinctive worship centres, the Blessed Chinese Martyrs Mission demonstrates what can happen when a church works at being a spiritual family.

The pastor, the Reverend Paul Tang, says the membership is large because people want fellowship. All the parishioners are of Chinese origin. Markham holds one of the Greater Toronto Area's six Chinatowns, but many parishioners come from farther afield to find community with people of their own culture. Each Sunday, there are four masses in Cantonese, one in Mandarin, and one in English.

Everything at this church seems big. In 1987 Sunday attendance was 260. By 1996 it was 4,000. There is now seating for 960. The clergy are assisted by 26 lay ministers in administering the Holy Communion. Seven choirs sing each weekend. The parking lot holds 120 cars, and a local school lot accommodates 180 more. Of the parishioners 60% are under 35 years of age, and at the English-language mass, 90%. Since the church opened in 1987, there have been 4,000 infant baptisms.

Adult baptisms are also frequent, with 300 men and women belonging to the RCIA (Rite of Christian Initiation of Adults) program, which is instructed by 60 lay volunteers.

Some of these are lapsed Roman Catholics who want to renew their faith, but many are converts from other religions such as Buddhism, and from secularism. What brings them to this church?

Some conversions result from the influence of an active church member in the family, and some people are attracted because they are lonely and need friends. Paul points to the great need for belonging among Chinese Canadians. Driving out to Markham is no obstacle when good fellowship is waiting at the end of the trip.

The church has built an activity centre with a library as well as meeting and conference rooms at a cost of $300,000, and maintains an annual budget of $500,000. When the centre was built, a new shrine to the Blessed Virgin Mary was incorporated into the worship centre — a sign that however important human fellowship is, the deepest personal needs we have are spiritual.

What message does this pentagon pattern offer?

❑ **Priorization of growth**

Instead of treating growth as an ancillary interest, growth churches understand that growth is intrinsic to the body of Christ. They know that an organism cannot stay alive without growth. Growth is always at the top of the agenda, right up there with the other essentials. Jesus' parable of the lost sheep reminds us that adding even one new member is growth.

❑ **Responsiveness to people's needs**

Growth churches shape their programs in response to needs people are feeling, rather than expecting people to accept a program that they lay on. Church life is more a "bottom-up" development than a "top-down" proclamation. Clergy and lay leaders carry on continual dialogue with people to ensure that real needs are identified and met.

❑ **Quality**

Doing everything in a quality way is essential for growth. It includes worship, music, preaching, buildings, pastoral care, education — everything a church is about.

Quality is not the special preserve of big, rich city churches. It means doing the best possible job with the resources available. It means taking time and paying attention to details. What it demands is not wealth but dedication. It is impossible to conceive that Jesus was a sloppy workman in Joseph's carpenter shop.

❏ Creativity

Doing what it takes to create growth requires imagination and creativity. This creativity is evident in many of the churches we have been visiting in this book, where clergy and laity have risen to challenges with fresh thinking.

Change is not an end in itself, but neither is resisting change. Maintaining a tradition often demands as much thought, imagination, and effort as initiating an innovation.

❏ Personal touch

People get lost in the crowds of life. At church, nothing ever replaces the personal touch as an outward and visible sign of the inward and spiritual grace that a church is dedicated to transmitting.

In a small church, people will not be lost in the crowd, but some small churches prefer the comfort of the known to the demands of the unknown in the form of new members with new views and new needs. The personal touch is needed there, too.

In a large church, people feel the personal touch when they are warmly welcomed as visitors. Most eventually find their place in a small group who listen to them and provide welcome human support. Even the largest church is made up of individuals drawn to a God who knows their names.

Chapter 5

Important as content is, growth depends more on style

Calgary's Jubilee Christian Centre, the Muskoka Christian Fellowship, St. John's Harwood, Mississauga's St. John of the Cross, and all the other churches we have visited so far offer a wide variety of styles of worship. The gospel message is clear in each one, but the style of presentation is strikingly different.

The Acts of the Apostles show that the early church had to accept differences of style if it was to fulfil its divine commission by penetrating the world of the Gentiles. In the Middle Ages, the style of the Dominicans was a world away from that of the Franciscans. In the sixteenth century, when Europe's newly reformed national churches failed to meet the needs of people who wanted other styles of worship, new sects emerged to meet them. Even fierce methods of coercion could not press Christians into the same mould.

When we worship God, we transcend the world, but we do not leave it. There cannot be a purely supernatural Christianity any more than there can be purely supernatural Christians. Nature is always the earthen vessel in which the gospel's heavenly treasure is contained. The vessel comes in different shapes: a charismatic revival and solemn high mass; electric guitars and Anglican chant; a rousing sermon and silent meditation; hands clapping and hands making the sign of the cross.

No one of these is right and the others wrong. Behind them lies the same desire to worship the same God, the same commitment to the same Lord, the same belief in the same Spirit. Different people respond to different ways of presenting the same gospel. In fact, the way the gospel is presented draws many more people to a church than matters of doctrine, ecclesiology, and morality do. Such matters are important. But they are not the missionary face of the church that welcomes inquirers and newcomers.

What attracts people is a church's distinctive style. There is a remarkable degree of agreement from church to church on the content of the Christian message. Churches do not dilute the gospel when they respect people's need for a particular style of presenting it, nor are they making a concession to the depravity of fallen human nature. We have different styles of learning, styles of leadership, styles of conflict resolution. Not surprisingly, we need different styles of preaching, of music, of worship. In fact, the style a church adopts is a sign of its respect for the humanity of people.

But by selecting one way rather than another, a church is likely to include some people and exclude others. Loud rock music will draw some. Gregorian chant and polyphony will draw others. Some will immediately recognize the divine presence by clapping and bursting into spontaneous laughter. Others will recognize God's presence by making the sign of the cross at the mention of the Holy Trinity. Those who respond to the one are unlikely to be able to share the same ecclesiastical tent with those who respond to the other. Yet a visitor might well think, "This is not where I want to come to worship every Sunday, but clearly it is where other people want to come."

Most of the churches we have visited both grow and maintain their integrity by being true to one particular way of presenting the gospel. Let us visit another quite different from the rest.

Toronto Airport Christian Fellowship is better known by its unofficial name, "the Toronto Blessing," which tells us how this unique centre grabbed hold of world interest and still draws people from faraway places.

In 1994 what seemed just one more evangelistic enterprise was launched on the outskirts of blasé, couldn't-care-less, we've-seen-it-all Toronto. The city had hosted Billy Graham, the Archbishop of Canterbury, the Dalai Lama, and Pope John Paul II. There was not the slightest reason to assume someone called Randy Clark, pastor of a charismatic church in St. Louis, Missouri, could affect the city when he came to address meetings at the Toronto congregation pastored by John Arnott.

By most standards, John and his wife, Carol, had achieved impressive results. But the Arnotts wanted to make a further in-depth difference, and hoped Randy's visit could start it. They could not have predicted what would happen.

People were converted. Believers renewed commitments. But many manifested their inward and spiritual responses in outward and visible signs. Some burst out laughing and could not stop. Some fell down on the floor and lay prostrate as if in a trance. Some jerked their heads up and down involuntarily. Some groaned. Some shouted at the top of their voices.

Unusual these phenomena might have been, but all of them can be found in scripture or history. Few in the media, however, knew that history. Reporters swarmed in and told the world about the sustained laughter. Soon seekers were arriving from all over Canada and the United States, but also from Europe, Asia, Africa, and Latin America.

Within the first seven months following the initial revival, the church's meetings had attracted a cumulative total of 90,000 persons, including 4,000 from 16 countries. By January 1999 the cumulative total for five years of activity had soared to three million.

One who came was Guy Chevreau, a tall and lithe doctor of theology as much at home on a surf board as in a library. Joining the staff that soon expanded to 70, including 15 ministers, Guy took on regular conferences for pastors and leaders and wrote three books in two years to tell the story of "the Toronto Blessing." He defends it against conservative critics even among evangelicals, claiming that it fits into the history of revivals that throughout the centuries have called Christians to renewal — the Methodist and the Welsh revivals, for example.

But it is the present that must count, and what a present it is, as we can see from a Tuesday night visit when people gathered in an upper room. About 30 people were seated in front of a blank wall with a pulldown screen and a microphone. The action had already begun. A woman was in visible dialogue with two men in the front row. When they laid hands on her head and prayed, she slowly sank to the floor where she lay for the rest of the evening as though in a faint. In contrast, one of the men was shouting when he was not groaning, and the other waved his hands back and forth, smiling without actually looking at anyone.

One of the staff took the microphone, flanked by a guitarist and a drummer. She explained that we were to intercede for revival throughout the world. Soon prayers were being offered for 16 countries as well as Canada and "the Ojibway nation." Most of the praying was done in songs whose words were cast on the screen. While they sang, people swayed and danced. Numbers grew until more chairs had to be brought in. By the end of the meeting 150 people had gathered. How many churches could claim a weekday prayer meeting of that size? Or report a regular Sunday evening service of over 500?

Sunday worship is in the stadium-sized main sanctuary equipped with green upholstered chairs facing a platform unadorned except for a large rough wooden cross that hangs against green drapes, some baskets of greenery, keyboards, drums, and guitars. The dynamic is audial, not visual: powerful, rhythmic, pulsating sound. As soon as the music starts, people are on their feet singing, swaying, waving, dancing. Most are between 20 and 40. But not all. A senior citizen from Oklahoma explains that she has been brought by her daughter to Toronto expressly to visit this church. Hers is not the only gray head.

Six songs are sung before a pastor, as casually dressed as most of the worshippers, takes a microphone and thanks God for loving us "not from a distance but up close." As he invites the ministry team to gather round the platform, he assures people they can look forward to miracles happening then and there. To support this claim, he reads three testimonial letters from people who had come to other services with needs and left with blessings.

The message fits a church whose staff end each conversation with "Bless you" — even at the bookstore cash register. It also fits a generation looking for something to satisfy their inner lives. Few churches may want to provide for those inner needs the way the Toronto Airport Christian Fellowship does, but every church must address them.

Although most churches select and maintain one particular way of presenting the gospel, some manage to accommodate members with radically different preferences for the way the gospel is presented.

Surrounded by high-rise office and condo buildings, St. Paul's Anglican on Toronto's Bloor Street East is one of the largest church buildings in the country. Built in 1913, it can seat 2,500, and it is large enough for great occasions like the visit of a pope or the funeral of a premier.

In a rich gothic sanctuary, a visitor expects to find a respect for tradition, a commitment to the majesty and grandeur of God expressed in ceremony and liturgy as well as art and architecture. A visitor is not disappointed. St. Paul's 60-voice robed choir and the preacher's sermon from a high, carved wooden pulpit both signify St. Paul's strong sense of tradition.

There are the usual ways for showing that people matter: greeters at the doors with their names on lapel tags, a warm welcome from the rector, the Reverend Dr. Barry Parker, before the service begins, the congregation being invited to shake hands with one another, a crowded coffee hour after the service ends.

In the pews are copies of both the old and the new Anglican liturgical books: the *Book of Common Prayer* and the *Book of Alternative Services*. But for anyone who finds these books awkward to use, there is a handsome booklet containing a simplified version of the orders of worship. That St. Paul's needs both the new rite and the old shows that liturgy is not mummified tradition but is constantly being recreated. It also shows that St. Paul's caters to different preferences in style of worship.

But St. Paul's readiness to change is demonstrated in a bolder act. Aware that the services were not attracting as many younger people as he wanted, William Hockin, a former rector who is now Co-adjutor Bishop of Fredericton, conceived "Worship in a New Key" to meet the needs of people for whom both liturgies were too unfamiliar or too formal.

Prudently, Bill made no changes in the existing services. Instead, he sandwiched the new one between the eight o'clock Holy Communion and the 11 o'clock. Parishioners thus had a choice, but without losing anything they wanted to keep.

Those who come at 9:15 a.m. experience Anglican worship as they may never have known it. Instead of being scattered in the nave, they gather in the chancel, a 20-voice choir seated at the foot of the steps around a piano. Most people come in sweaters and slacks; even the clergy are only in suits. The eucharist is articulated in reverential but contemporary language. The communion vessels are earthenware, not silver, and plain bread replaces wafers. The music is especially composed by the church's choir director, Eric Robertson, and a parishioner, Richard Ouzounian, who is also a television writer. Communicants are conscious of God present in each other as well as in the sacrament. The content is old-time religion but the style is now-time.

The service has a steady clientele, and rather than reducing numbers at the other, traditional services, it has increased total Sunday attendance. When Bill Hockin moved to New Brunswick to become Dean of Fredericton, he did the same thing all over again at Christ Church Cathedral, and the new service has been welcomed in that tradition-conscious part of Canada, too.

In today's world, people want options. No one style of worship appeals to everyone. A church may concentrate on its single distinctive style and grow like the Toronto Blessing. Or it may manage different styles at different services and attract people the way St. Paul's Bloor Street does.

The gospel message is the same forever and everywhere. But a concern for style is imperative.

A message about a growth-priority style

❑ **People today want options. No style of worship has uniform appeal. Churches grow when**
• they opt for a particular style of presenting the gospel that appeals to many people, *or*
• they make room for a choice of styles in which the gospel is presented.

Either way, they grow when they emphasize and perfect a style of worship, preaching, and music.

None of this is new. Nor does a focus on style dilute the integrity of a church and turn it from sincerity to fakery. Nor does it mean that the content of the gospel message is unimportant.

What it does mean is that, when a church selects a particular style, it is respecting people's humanity.

Chapter 6

Churches sustain growth not by gimmicks but by their quality of life

Church people ask, "What will bring people to our church?" and "What will bring them back?" But even more important is the question, "What will keep them coming?" Clever "gimmicks" may help to answer the first question, maybe even the second. But only the quality of a church's life will lead newcomers from being uncommitted attenders to becoming participating members.

To see what that means in experience, let us focus on two essential qualities of churches that are sustaining their growth: excellence and integrity.

Excellence

Excellence is one explanation for how the United Church of Canada's largest congregation goes on bringing a thousand worshippers together most Sundays. In London, Ontario, Metropolitan United stays up top by offering the best.

Built in 1896, it can seat 1,250, and a century later, it still fills most of those seats. In a time when many large churches are showing more wood than people, this record demands some explaining. At first sight, Metropolitan could be almost any other Protestant place of worship. Its order of service goes back to the basic pattern of synagogue worship in pre-Christian times: singing the praises of God, hearing his word read and expounded, offering thanksgivings and prayers. The massed adult choir faces the congregation seated not only on the main floor but in a sweep around gallery. Worship is conducted from a pulpit and a lectern on either side of the choir by ministers robed in Reformation-era black gowns instead of the coloured ones favoured by many clergy today.

In an age of change, not much has changed at Metropolitan. That may be one of the reasons why so many people come — seeking from the church something to stabilize their lives, to give them order, to count on. Significantly, Metropolitan belongs to the conservative Association of Covenanted Churches.

But many other churches that have not changed and that have taken conservative doctrinal positions are almost empty. What makes the difference at Metropolitan is that what it does, it does very, very well. The conventional wisdom in London holds that Metropolitan is the place to find good sermons and good music. The crowds show how many people are attracted to traditional Christianity when it is presented with excellent quality.

The current minister, the Reverend Robert Ripley, leads the way. Preparing his sermon shapes his week. By Tuesday noon, he knows its theme and has a title ready for the printing of the Sunday bulletin. Wednesday is devoted to pastoral visiting, by which he both serves people's needs and learns what their concerns are. Thursday and Friday are devoted to writing and rewriting the message that has been percolating all week in order to have a completed script by Friday noon. Part of Saturday is spent committing the sermon to memory, so that in the pulpit it can flow as spontaneously as if the preacher had just thought it up. Just to make sure it does, he spends an hour alone in his study on Sunday morning rehearsing it one more time.

Himself one of the baby-boomer generation, Bob senses its priorities, adapting both message and delivery to them. His sermons bear titles like "Seven Steps to a Better Home," and "St. Irma Bombeck." When he speaks, a microphone attached to his gown permits him to deliver his sermon in a tone more conversational than "preachy."

Although the sermon is central, it is only part of the Metropolitan experience. In a city accustomed to quality music, this church is a place for music lovers to go. Concert-quality organ recitals precede and follow the service. The 120-voice choir, led by the church's brilliant music director, Brent Hylton, and his wife, Marilyn, sing two anthems during the service. A children's choir is often involved, too.

The staff includes a full-time minister of Christian education, Margaret Scott, who with her army of volunteers marshalls 180 children in the Sunday school, often addressing them with a children's homily as part of the church's worship before they go to classes. That their special children's programs are top quality is clear from the fact that the annual Christmas Eve family service is a standing-room-only event.

When he was the assistant minister, the Reverend Douglas Storey devoted himself full time to pastoral care and to training lay volunteers to help him. Twelve small groups are alive and well. A monthly men's breakfast continues to draw large numbers, as do organizations for women and seniors. An annual series of various interest activities and study topics attracts people from throughout the London area. An Out of the Cold ministry is maintained for street people. Constructing a Habitat for Humanity house is also a church project.

Metropolitan's quality presentation of a traditional church program clearly suits a city accustomed to quality and tradition. Will it be enough though for the future? Nothing in the twenty-first century is guaranteed. But Metropolitan is meeting the challenge by striving to take in enough new members — at least 100 a year — to compensate for the unavoidable loss of people through death and changing membership. It is also maintaining the annual budget needed to keep up its staffing and programming.

Integrity

A church is more likely to enjoy sustained growth when it has defined itself as the kind of fellowship it wants to be and has a clear sense of direction.

All Saints' Anglican in Regina appeals to people wanting a church with a stress on participation and an opportunity to think about their faith. Its rector, the Venerable Gary Paterson, stresses consensus decision making, so that people share in group life by sharing group decisions and have a sense of ownership of their church and its policies. When the Anglican Church of Canada approved a new liturgy, the *Book of Alternative Services*, Gary did not force it on people, but respected their right to choose between it and the *Book of Common Prayer* with its centuries-old language beloved by so many Anglicans. He also respected the choice they made: to have both in the one church.

All Saints' also attracts people who want priority given to education. Most of them have at least one university degree. One mother joined when she called the Anglican diocesan headquarters and bluntly asked the name of the church with the best Sunday school in town. Directed to All Saints', she loaded her family into the van even though it meant driving past a much closer Anglican church. To serve its enrolment of 100 children, the school has 20 volunteer teachers, each one alternating with another so that no teacher misses the worship every Sunday morning.

Adult education matters, too. At All Saints', people dare to disagree and to think new thoughts. A women's group announced at a Sunday morning eucharist that its study group would discuss a new book on myths about the birth of Christ. If anyone was shocked, they didn't show it.

The church provides training programs for Sunday school teachers and other lay leadership offices, even for the job of greeting people on Sunday morning. It has no specific growth program but relies on word-of-mouth recommendations. When a senior academic and his wife and children moved into town, they heard at a cocktail party that All Saints' was a good place for people like them, and although they had been members of another denomination, they tried it out, liked what they found, and are still coming.

Can All Saints' continue to generate enough sustaining growth to replace inevitable annual losses? Gary, confident it can, points to how, since the 1991 building expansion that cost $400,000, the parish roll has lengthened from 300 to 350 families, and Sunday attendance has risen to more than 200 adults and children. There is a place, he says, for the medium-sized church like All Saints'; one that stands between a pastoral size where there can be a one-on-one relationship and a program size where people find fellowship in groups and organizations.

Both Metropolitan United and All Saints' enjoy sustained growth because they have defined themselves and remain true to themselves, even as they adapt to changing circumstances. For any church to sustain growth it has to remember Jesus' parable of the talents. No church has all the talents; some may have only one. But when even one talent is used to the full, the Lord's mission for that church is being served.

The message is give priority to quality

❑ Sustaining growth is every bit as challenging as undertaking it in the first place.
Clever "gimmicks" are not likely to have perennial appeal.

❑ Some changes may not be possible.
For example, at Metropolitan United, there is very little reception space at the entrance to the church where newcomers can be welcomed, and people can stop to chat. Instead, everyone has to move to the gym after the service.

❑ Not all change is good.
When a church already has a winning style of worship that packs people in as at Metropolitan, there is no immediate need for change.

❑ But avoiding all change can be dangerous.
A church must never ignore people's needs nor allow itself to go out of date in relation to their needs.

❑ To sustain growth, a church must maintain excellence in all it does.
Once a church is assured that it is on the right track in serving its people, it can be assured of sustaining growth when it maintains excellence in all it does.

❑ **It must maintain its integrity.**

No church can be all things to all people. Each church needs self-definition and a sense of its own direction. That extends to selecting both clergy and lay leaders who are at home with the direction the church is taking.

Chapter 7

Creative planning makes use of demographic change to ensure growth

B usiness is not the only activity affected by demographics, as the impact of population change is called. Since John Gaunt's seventeenth-century study of baptisms and deaths showed England how many men of military age its leaders could expect, demographics have been seen as a vital factor in history — including church life.

Churches are shaped and reshaped by such demographic factors as age, gender, ethnic origin, and marital status as well as birth, death, and movement. For example, the Anglican Church of Canada grew from 1895 to 1965 through the immigration of people who had been members of the Church of England. The Orthodox Church is growing right now through immigration from post-communist eastern Europe.

Some local churches come into being because housing developments fill empty fields with family homes. Big changes occur in others when immigrants from the same homeland arrive in the neighbourhood.

We have already visited churches that have experienced cyclical growth as the result of changed demographics. But cyclical growth may be terminated once families mature, grown-up children leave, and parents age, or when the ethnic composition of the neighbourhood changes, or when a major employer closes down and people have to move elsewhere to find work. Churches sustain growth when their quality of life attracts people and holds them.

A church can even create its own community in response to changing demographics.

In north-west Toronto, St. Hilda's Anglican created a community when it built three high-rise apartment towers for seniors on its adjacent property, then tore down its worship centre and built a new one as part of a fourth tower. Having lost most of the old congregation, it created a new one.

The Reverend Canon Clifford Ward saw a need and an opportunity when money for the construction of seniors' residences became available through the Ontario government. Not every declining church can or should be transformed this way. What Cliff and St. Hilda's show is how decline is not inevitable if demographic change and creativity can be married to each other.

St. Hilda's neighbourhood was first settled by British immigrants before and after World War I. When they built a church, they erected one in a Tudor design that was a bit of old England in stucco and lathe.

Financially all but devastated by the Depression of the 1930s, the church was saved by the arrival of an uncommon man, the Reverend Canon Albert Jackson, known to everyone as Bert. Part of the budget crisis was solved by bachelor Bert living in a room in the church and taking no salary. After World War II, in which he served as a chaplain, Bert stirred up support for tearing the old building down and replacing it with a unique, all-concrete structure in the shape of a parabolic arch. Bert said he had always dreamed of putting a distinctly Canadian church where the distinctly English one had stood, and when some critic complained that his new building looked like an igloo, Bert replied: "Thank you very much."

A lesser man than Clifford Ward might have felt threatened when he succeeded Bert, especially when Bert stayed on as honorary assistant, but they were two of a kind and quickly formed a partnership that would prove essential to making St. Hilda's Towers a reality. Soon one, then two apartment towers rose and quickly were filled with mainly WASP seniors ready to come to a church that was just next door.

But when the igloo church showed structural faults and needed major renovation, the cost was beyond the capability of a membership comprised now of seniors in the towers and people in the neighbourhood whose parents had come from the Caribbean as immigrants. Putting up apartment towers with government funding was one thing. Rebuilding a worship centre with inadequate contributions was something else.

At a congregational meeting Cliff promised to replace the old church with a new one without asking the people for a cent. Astounded and incredulous as many were, the congregation accepted his dare, not knowing what he had up his sleeve.

With government funding, he was able to erect a third tower, and then he sold the church's air rights, so that he could build a new church incorporated into the apartment complex. He even negotiated a sizable cash settlement with an oil company whose service station had polluted St. Hilda's property. The project cost over $2-million, but the parishioners had to finance only the cost of furnishing the new sanctuary.

Low-rise and square-shaped, with its pews arranged in three banks around a chancel set in one corner, this place of worship is dominated by eight gloriously multicoloured windows that reach from floor to ceiling. It is shiny with newness, rich with colour, alive with people.

Sunday attendance of 250, composed mainly of white seniors and Caribbean families, is triple what St. Hilda's was attracting before the new church was built. The Caribbean people had mostly moved to Toronto's suburbs and could have been lost, but they were drawn back and today form 60% of the church's attendance and almost all its leadership. Why? They love the new church with its colourful beauty. They love seeing one another on Sundays after having been scattered all week. They also love Cliff, this growth church like most others being a wheel that turns around its clerical hub.

That strength, however, can be a weakness when it comes time for a pastor to leave, and Cliff has now retired. Fortunately for St. Hilda's, a new rector with a proven track record in serving both church and community has been appointed to carry on. He is the Reverend Derwin Shea, who has spent more than 28 years serving an inner city parish and many years as a provincial legislator and municipal councillor.

The message is that demographic change can be a new opportunity

St. Hilda's was worth our visit not only because of its own story but because of its pointing out features of growth that demand forward planning.

Cyclical growth can be as thrilling as surf riding when the demographic curve lifts a church up and carries it forward. But just as the surf tips its rider on the beach, so the demographic curve can spell decline for a church. It does just that when the people who once filled every pew move, age, or die. Nothing is forever, including buoyant population growth.

When demographic change thus goes against a church, the temptation is to give up. But there is no need to yield to that temptation.

What Cliff Ward did at St. Hilda's may be impossible to copy exactly. But it shows that decline is not the only option. Creative thinking may reveal other possibilities. Demographic change has been part of Christian history since a Roman census determined where Jesus would be born, and it is inescapably part of Christian life today. Responding to it takes creativity, energy, determination, and a lot of planning.

Chapter 8

New churches emerge when old ones fail to meet needs

Christ's incarnation tells us that God loves our humanity. We are not just spiritual beings; we are flesh and blood, too. When churches, through indifference, preoccupation, or choice, ignore people's flesh and blood needs, new churches will emerge to satisfy them.

We have already visited several churches across Canada that have arisen in response to needs not being met by existing churches, but let us focus on two more that show how widely differing needs can lead to the same emergent response.

On a cold, icebound December Sunday in Toronto, people are filing into the massive edifice in large numbers. Inside, casually dressed worshippers greet each other warmly, and newcomers are welcomed not only by official greeters but by one church member after another. There is a good feeling; people are glad to be here. But this church is unique. Most of its people are gays and lesbians. It is the Metropolitan Community Church of Toronto.

A married couple, surprised to see my wife, Margaret, and me ask, "What are you doing here?" They are old friends and I reply, "I was just going to ask you the same question." They tell me they have a gay son who comes to this church and they have come to support him. So have parents, friends, and relatives of other members of the church, and the congregation now includes more than the gays and lesbians for which it was formed. They now have their own fellowship, Parents and Families of Lesbians and Gays (PFLAG), which meets twice a month, once in a Presbyterian church and once in an Anglican one.

Unlike most congregations, where most worshippers are women, men are the majority here. Otherwise the worship could be found in any Protestant church. A robed choir processes into stalls that face the people, followed by two gowned ministers, one a woman, one a man, each wearing a purple stole for the Advent season.

The Reverend Brent Hawkes welcomes the congregation, but looking at some empty seats, asks: "Where is everyone? They must be coming to the Christmas Carol Service tonight." Yet there are 400 worshippers present, more than you would find in most Protestant churches in Toronto's inner city, and you know they are there when all those male voices rise up in praise.

The service follows a traditional order of invocation, psalm, scripture, prayer, offering, announcements, and a sermon, punctuated by hymns, a solo, and an anthem. We could be anywhere. The sermon, too, is a biblically based message about Christ. Neither in the sermon nor in the announcements is there any reference to sexual orientation. But one announcement informs the congregation that because the Christmas Eve service is so popular, it is held at Toronto's Roy Thomson Hall, and they had better reserve their seats early. Last year over 200 people had to be turned away.

The climax of the service is Holy Communion when almost everyone kneels at the communion rail and receives the sacrament by intinction; that is, the wafer is dipped in the wine and then placed on the tongue. For those who wish a special blessing, unction with oil is offered to 80 persons who kneel for it. The ministers anoint them in turn, listen to their personal need, and offer prayer for them. It is a pastoral moment, an act of caring and sharing.

What brought this church into being was that many gays and lesbians did not find their needs being met in the historic denominations. One gay man, Troy Perry, decided to do something about it and formed what has now become a new denomination, the Metropolitan Community Church (MCC). It has 300 churches, mostly in the United States.

The Toronto church was founded by Brent Hawkes, who, raised a Baptist in New Brunswick, did not want to abandon his faith when he "came out." Instead he studied at the Toronto School of Theology, graduating in 1985 and being ordained that year. By then he had already been the lay pastor of the Toronto MCC congregation while still working as an insurance underwriter.

From its small beginning with 50 members in 1977, it became large enough for Brent to begin a full-time ministry and to purchase an unused United Church building. But numbers kept growing and the church was forced to buy a still larger sanctuary. It, too, is at capacity now and a second morning service is being considered. Brent's own dream is to erect a brand-new church with an apartment complex for gay seniors. When asked if the dream is possible, Brent replies, "With God, no dream is impossible." He can back up his faith with an annual budget of $826,000.

Brent is a man always ready for ventures of faith, such as renting Roy Thomson Hall for Christmas Eve, so that more people can be accommodated to celebrate the festival. Brent's faith was vindicated when one couple put up $22,000 to pay the rent. The service was a hit from the start. Seats now go for $10 each and totally sell out, so that the service pays for itself.

Brent also knows what quality is. At that Christmas service, a 75-voice choir makes it a night to remember. The worship reaches deep into the hearts of this congregation when all who have lost someone in the previous 12 months are invited to stand. Most do, many of them mourning loved ones who have died of AIDS.

With seven other gay and lesbian churches across Canada and more likely to form, historic denominations with a tradition of rejecting homosexual practice as an acceptable option for Christians are faced with a dilemma. Since gays and lesbians will not go away, should these denominations expand their pastoral horizons or remain committed to their centuries-old teaching?

One thing is clear: no one can just be shut out. If the doors of one church are closed to people with a need, they will either find one with open doors or build one themselves. In today's open society, they do not even have to go underground the way suppressed groups had to do in the past.

They can start up on their own the way a Winnipeg group did with a need totally different from accommodating alternative sexualities.

One of the features of today's emerging growth churches is their propensity to choose names different from the customary saints' or community names. We have already learned some of them, but could any be more distinctive than Grain of Wheat Church Community?

Just as in biblical times people believed a name denoted a character, so new churches often choose names that will affirm what they are. This name declares that out of dying to accepted social values, a new life can be born. It also expresses the hope that this church will be a community in which people share their lives.

It began in 1981 when 20 Winnipeg people, all frustrated with the shallowness of their culture and the constraints of their church experiences, decided to form a church community of their own. They wanted one committed to serving social justice, and some of the members committed themselves to moving into a lower-income neighbourhood where they would not serve from above, but share the lives of their fellow human beings. They also wanted one where church members as a community would shape their common life instead of receiving it from the top down.

One of these people was Dr. James Krahn, a physician who, like some of the others, moved with his wife and children into a neighbourhood with whose residents they hoped to identify. It was not the kind of residential community where medical doctors and other professionals usually live, and that was the point. He and others were making an effort to transcend the usual income-based divisions that fragment today's urban communities. Dr. Krahn testifies that he discovered his own poverty through living and working among the poor.

The original 20 met for worship in a private home, but not for long. When their numbers grew beyond that space, they had to move to a United Church basement for regular worship, and they offered a healing ministry at a Roman Catholic church. Grain of Wheat now has 50 members and 100 adherents, but some occasions bring 200 worshippers together.

A typical Sunday begins with teaching for adults as well as children, followed by worship that includes singing, preaching, and Holy Communion. The liturgies of various traditions are used for this worship, including the *Book of Common Prayer* for the Holy Communion, as well as free worship prepared by the members themselves. Once a month they share a common meal. On alternate Wednesdays, they meet as small groups of six to nine for closer fellowship with one another, sometimes over a meal.

In the church's early years, priority was given to social action with prayer vigils, peace marches, demonstrations, and refugee relief, but there is less emphasis on that now just as there is in society generally.

Leadership of the church is provided by a team of members, one giving pastoral care, another leading the worship, and another doing administration. They are paid half-time salaries and usually work at something else, too. They have served for varying terms, from one to ten years.

This church is home-grown with a bottom-up structure different from the top-down structure of most denominations. If these modern Canadian Christians sound something like the people who followed St. Francis centuries ago, it is not by accident. Their kind of commitment is needed in any age of history. Just as St. Francis's religious order emerged from medieval Christianity, so the Grain of Wheat community has emerged today. When other churches fail to provide for this kind of commitment, concerned people will step in and do it themselves.

The message is clear: needs will be met

Those who believe that a top-down structure is divinely ordained for the church may be disturbed by the fecundity of Christian life, which generates bottom-up structures to fill needs that the established denominations do not meet.

The established denominations have only two options:

• They can ignore this evolution and let the new Christian communities live and possibly thrive on their own.

• They can accommodate this evolution within themselves, making room for what they could have conceived but failed to.

Once we accept the implications of believing that like the wind, the Holy Spirit will blow where he will, we can see Christianity in bottom-up terms. We can welcome new movements within our own churches, and welcome new churches that emerge to a wider Christian fellowship.

This infinite Christian capacity for evolving new ways of finding salvation should inspire thanksgiving. In Canada, it is part of the Christian recovery story.

Chapter 9

We need fewer churches but more ministries

1. The priority is shifting from churches to ministries

Among my earliest memories as a child is walking to church on Sundays. Almost no one drove a car to church or used public transit. Although I did not realize it, I was part of a long tradition that was about to end. A church then had to be within easy walking distance. "Brand loyalty" to the denomination was strong enough that people would remain faithful as long as a church was "walkable." People did not expect top-quality services in times when they had little with which to compare their local church except the local churches of other denominations. Proximity was the key.

Everything has changed. People today drive to meet almost every need — and sometimes for very long distances. Children may be bused to another neighbourhood for school. Parents may commute to another city or town for work. Families ignore distance to pursue bargain prices at discount stores. People will travel just as far on Sunday to find the spiritual satisfaction they are seeking.

That the denomination of their ancestors has a church two blocks from home may not matter if a church 10 miles away has the preaching or music or education or other ministry they want. In the pedestrian era, the term "parish" made sense as a way of describing the area around a church building that its clergy served. But a church can seldom prosper now just by being based on a community of space. To grow, it must provide a community of interest.

Few of our experiences are space oriented. On the same street, few people work for the same company. Few share the same interests or recreational activities. Few may even see each other except in passing on the street itself. Why should any of them feel any special desire to attend a neighbourhood church?

You could argue that smaller local churches provide the personal fellowship denied to people in larger ones. But do they? Some churches are small because they deny fellowship to the stranger who comes within their walls. The reality is that a growth church is likely to be more welcoming and provide more fellowship because it has a mission-mentality. A welcome can be found in churches, large as well as small, that make groups part of their life, using these fellowship cells as a way of making sure that the personal touch is felt in the midst of the massive crowd. Critics of "bigness" are right when they stress the importance of fellowship, but they are wrong when they assume a big church cannot provide it and a small one always does.

Once we see that sharing the gospel with as many people as possible is part of the divine commission, then the issue ceases to be size. The focus becomes the stewardship of resources: how can we best use them to serve our mission on earth?

The word stewardship is often nothing more than a euphemism for church finances, a stewardship appeal usually meaning a campaign for regular giving. But when the New Testament speaks about the people of God having stewardship, it reflects the ancient understanding of a steward as a person who managed the resources of someone else. His duty was to see that the best use was made of them. Otherwise he was what Jesus called an "unprofitable servant." In a church, stewardship should now mean making the best use of facilities, finances, and people to serve God's purposes and the church's mission.

One implication is that achieving the objective of the church's divine commission may demand more ministries than the old one-man-band kind of church. And to assure quality, these ministries must be managed by skilled personnel with time and resources to do the job.

A single cleric can seldom provide superior preaching on a regular basis when he or she is diverted by a host of other demands — recruiting Sunday school teachers, counselling the troubled, evangelizing the community, and so on. Choirs can seldom compare with what people can hear day after day on their own tape-decks if there is not a minister of music able to achieve a high standard of performance. When church members lament the lack of young people, they should ask themselves if it is time to employ a youth minister. Pastoral care may actually be better in a large church where a minister is exclusively devoted to it, than in a small or medium-sized church where a solitary pastor must add it to all the other duties.

We live in a society of specialization, yet even in New Testament times and for centuries afterward, specialized ministries played their part in the life of the church. The New Testament list of ministers is a long one: apostles, bishops, presbyters, elders, deacons, evangelists, teachers, pastors, prophets, widows. Each of them had a defined ministry to perform, and each was respected as a minister of Christ. Together they got the job done.

As the church evolved, some of those New Testament ministries passed out of its life, but were replaced by others. Through the time of the early church fathers and into the Middle Ages, seven orders of the ministry were recognized; four of them — porter, exorcist, acolyte, and reader — were called "minor orders." In the English Reformation of the sixteenth century the seven were reduced to three: bishop, priest, and deacon. In the Calvinist Reformation, those three were merged into one, simply called "the minister."

But in growth churches Christians are returning to that earlier pattern of many ministries, each with its own "job description," each with its own dignity. The test of the effectiveness of these ministries is whether they are helping the church to "steward" its resources on behalf of its Lord.

As the priority shifts to ministries, buildings take on less importance. A night club or a cinema or a rented hotel meeting room can serve for worship. Little attention may be paid to decoration, atmosphere, ornamentation, or visual symbols. As in the Bible, the focus will be less on sight, more on sound — the ministry of the word preached or sung or taught.

Stewardship does not mean closing up all the small churches in order to supply members for the big ones. But closing some may free resources to be used more effectively. Closures and mergers should not be considered as economy measures, as ways of doing more with less, as ways of having just one worship centre, so that only one minister will be needed. Just the opposite. The need is for more ministries, clerical and lay; and if they can be supplied by reducing the number of church buildings, the decision to close a church should not be seen as a retreat from the days of former glory. It should be grasped as an advance to a time of new growth.

Understandably, church members resist the closing of their building and the end of their autonomy as a congregation. Old churches are full of memories, often in the tangible form of memorials to old friends and relatives. But postponing the closure of some churches holds up the mission of the greater church, which is better served by more ministries and fewer costly buildings. Closing a church may be the way for Christians to grasp their vocation as stewards of the grace God has given them.

An advancing army needs troops on the ground, but the troops need officers. Growth churches show that many of the officers do not need the old-style training of a university degree followed by three years in seminary. Many of them do not need to be ordained. Multiple ministries include ordained persons trained in the usual way, but a church administrator, a minister of music, a minister of youth may have quite different qualifications.

An underused resource in many churches is the retired clergy and laity. A church wanting to expand its ministry could make no better start than drafting an inventory of human resources. It might not have to move beyond its own membership to meet all its ministry needs once pastor and parishioners liberate themselves from the fixation that a church has only one "minister."

Growth churches approach their ministry needs by asking how they can best serve the mission of Christ. Once a church accepts that mission is its reason for existence, dealing with ministry becomes a matter of stewardship to make the best use of resources.

Back on the beautiful west coast, a big church shows the way of using multiple ministries to serve people's needs at a very personal level.

2. Grow more to serve more

"The Willingdon Church" is the very ordinary name of a very extraordinary Christian centre in the heart of Burnaby, an attractive community now part of Greater Vancouver lying beneath the towering peaks of the coastal range.

Like the office towers and mountains that mark Burnaby's horizon, everything about this church is outsize. With 4,000 members and adherents, it may be the largest Protestant church in western Canada. Its gross revenue of just over $3-million comes mainly from Sunday offerings large enough to require two armoured cars to take them to the bank. It has 16 pastors to serve over 3,000 worshippers a Sunday in eight languages.

All week long Willingdon works at that Sunday pace. Name a ministry and this church is probably providing it. Its program includes support groups for divorced persons, nursery school for young children, after-hours sports for teenagers, Bible study for 60 home-based small groups — to name only a few of its "full-service church" activities.

To keep it all going requires more volunteers than an ordinary church's entire membership. Laity are involved in every ministry from telephone counselling to organizing the parking lot. If you have a warm smile, your calling may be as a greeter who makes others feel welcome. If you're fluent in another language, you may be trained for simultaneous translation at some of the Sunday services. If you can cook, you can help with a dinner served after the second Sunday morning service or other meals and refreshments throughout the week.

What explains this bursting activity? Willingdon began in 1961 as a church planted by a Mennonite Brethren congregation in Vancouver, 115 charter members forming its original base. The new church took 10 years to double its numbers. Two pastors came and went. Then in 1972 Herb Neufeld arrived, and with him a vision of the great church Willingdon could become. His enthusiasm was contagious. It was said that people did not know what a hug was until they had been hugged by this pastor with a big frame and a big heart. He defined the term "people person." He laughed with people's joys and literally wept with them in their sorrows.

So Willingdon took off. Ten years after he arrived, the present immense sanctuary was built with seating for 1,400. The church's self-understanding expanded, too: it became a community church that welcomes all sorts and conditions of people. Although Herb was at the centre of all this, he was not the whole of it. One of his many initiatives was introducing the small group dimension to Willingdon's life, so that men and women could find spiritual direction and fellowship through home meetings and study programs. No growth church can be a wheel without a pastoral hub, but no hub can travel far without a wheel.

According to Bill Klassen, now senior assistant pastor for administration, Herb made another vital contribution. He stayed for 14 years. As we have seen elsewhere, long-term pastorates go with growth.

Herb's successor, Carlin Wienhauer, has been at Willingdon since 1984. As senior pastor, he occupies the pulpit on Sundays and takes his people through a kind of biblical course extending over several months with divergences to mark the great festivals of the Christian year. For example, he may preach most of the year on the gospel according to St. Mark.

Willingdon is now having to consider holding a third Sunday service to accommodate the increasing numbers. It has never split. Without diluting the clearly defined doctrinal and moral requirements of the Mennonite Brethren, it has grown beyond its denomination and yet avoided both tension and schism.

But it readily accommodates diversity. Its worship blends traditional and contemporary music, so that people of different ages and tastes can be served without anyone having to go elsewhere, or without fragmenting the church into largely segregated congregations.

Its program provides something for everybody, be it high school kids wanting gymnastics or senior citizens seeking fellowship and intellectual stimulation. Big as it is, Willingdon remains a place where very different people can feel equally at home. It accommodates its community's multicultural character with its multilanguage ministry. It may have been one of the very few Canadian churches to help the people of Chechnya when their country was invaded by Russian troops. After the monthly Holy Communion service, a "retiring" offering is received and devoted to the needy of the local Burnaby community. Willingdon also operates its own food bank.

Not surprisingly, this generosity to others does not weaken the church's ability to finance itself. The 1982 building expansion cost $5.8-million, but the debt has been brought down below $2-million, and the payments are now small enough to be absorbed into the regular budget. Its Sunday offerings are so large that two Brinks trucks are needed to take them to the bank.

Bigger is not always better, but Willingdon shows how bigger does not have to mean colder. It has grown because its big size includes a big heart. Size does not have to be the enemy of caring.

Here is a new message about an old truth

☐ Larger churches with more ministries may meet today's needs better than small churches with a single minister.

• A large church with more ministers can deliver special programs for the old, the young, young couples, the divorced, the bereaved, the sick, the poor, and many others with particular needs.

• Ministers will include lay people with various specialist qualifications as well as ordained clergy.

• Some ministers will be paid full-time workers, but the role of volunteers will also expand.

• Retired people, clerical and lay, are an underused resource.

☐ Large does not necessarily mean impersonal or unfriendly.

• Stewardship is making the best use of resources, human as well as financial.

• Growth churches develop programs for welcoming newcomers.

• Growth churches use small group ministries to ensure fellowship, care, and a sense of belonging.

Chapter 10

Signs of recovery after decades of recession

For several years, every winter morning I walked along my favourite beach on Florida's Gulf coast observing the tide line. You may ask what possible gospel there can be in a natural phenomenon so apparently uninspiring as the ebb and flow of the tides. But there is a message in the tides for the Canadian churches — and it's good news.

Throughout Christian history there have been periods of growth followed by times of recession, which in turn have given way to years of recovery.

In his monumental *History of the Expansion of Christianity*, Yale professor Kenneth Latourette traced this ebb and flow. In nature, when the tide is flowing, each wave comes in and then falls back, but each successive wave advances farther. In this way Christianity has expanded through more than 19 centuries, Latourette wrote, in a cycle of recessions and recoveries.

But Latourette was writing at mid-century. What would he write now? Were he still in this world, he could confidently claim the past 50 years have confirmed his prophetic description of this era as an advance through storm, a time of progress that has gone beyond anything that could have been anticipated. The number of Christians has grown as never before. Over 1.5 billion people profess the name of Jesus Christ — almost double the number in 1950. During the years in which Western Christians have been struggling to hold their own, the churches in what were once missionary lands have been exploding in growth.

There is another reason for Christian confidence, too. In countries where church attendance has spiralled down, the number of people still calling themselves Christian has remained impressively high. Contrary to the claim that nominal Christianity is meaningless, it should be seen as an opportunity. It is a point of contact between the churches and the so-called "unchurched."

Even in the midst of the trials and challenges, Christianity can assert that this half-century has been an advance through the storm, and if that storm has not abated, neither has the advance faltered. At the turn of the century the tide may be coming in as never before.

Can we make this claim for Canada, too? There are 10 signs that tell us recovery is near in this country, that the tide that went out in the mid-1950s is about to come in, that what ebbed then is ready to flood again now. There are signs that we are living not in the twilight of faith, but on the eve of its renewal.

1. Christianity is growing in the USA, and religion is displacing secularity all over the world. Can Canada be far behind?

Religious decline has bottomed out in the United States, and what happens there may be prophetic of what will happen here.

In 1990 an estimated 151,225,000 out of a total adult population of 175,440,000 Americans said they were Christians — 86%. Their Christianity is not just social custom without personal meaning. About one in three claims to be "born again," the evangelical movement among Protestants and the charismatic movement among Roman Catholics being among the growth trends in American religious life.

The United States may have more churches — 400,000 — than any other country in the world, all of them supported not by state funding or endowments from the past, but by the people who attend them. Some of these Christian centres are nothing less than astounding in the scope of their giving. The Saddleback Valley Community Church in Mission Yiego, California, plans to construct a complex that will cost an estimated $50-million. With 15,000 worshippers, Willow Creek, the best known of the country's 400 megachurches, has a payroll of 200 full-time employees. Just to keep it all going requires a dynamism that shows something superlative is happening in American Christianity.

American culture itself reflects a Christian presence. The expansion of privately funded Christian schools has been phenomenal. Equally impressive is the growth of Christian television, radio, and publishing. Even T-shirts with evangelical messages show God is not dead in America!

Given that ideas as well as goods trade freely across the Canada-United States border, the recovery of American Christianity can strengthen the same trend in Canada. The trend here is characteristically less dramatic, but it is not less real.

In the wider world, too, religion is expanding its influence, not retreating. Think of the influence of Christians such as Pope John Paul II, Bishop Desmond Tutu, and Billy Graham. Even the influence of leaders of other religions, positive as in the case of the Dalai Lama of Tibet, or negative as in the case of some Moslem, Hindu, and Christian extremists, is less a threat to Christianity than a sign that secularism has been tried and found wanting.

2. The media are devoting increasing attention to religion

More significant still is the growth of religion in the media's world of interest. Where religion drew a blank on ABC television's "World News Tonight" in 1977, it was given 4.2% of time in 1997 on the television news report most widely watched in the United States. *Time* magazine, which in 1977 no longer carried its once informative religion section, in 1997 devoted 7.7% of its space to religion, more than it gave to foreign affairs or personal health, and equal to the space it devoted to domestic affairs.

3. Everywhere in Western culture there is a renewed interest in spirituality

Spirituality is recognized as a necessary dimension of a full life, something to be sought if one wants to be truly human. Secularity is out and spirituality is in.

It takes many forms. It may inspire corporate seminars and retreats that deal with psychology more than theology. It may probe the depths of existence without reference to the supernatural at all. It may draw people to New Age writers and speakers whose teaching provides an alternative to Christianity — a faith tailor-made for a new age that seems to deal with the inner person but nothing beyond the person.

But churches do not have to recoil defensively from these non-Christian forms of spirituality. When the gospel was introduced to pagan Europe, pagan customs were often more a bridge to the gospel than a barrier. When people are seeking spiritual refreshment, they may be as open to the church's message as to any other. Sadly, some have tried the churches and found only a dead past. They need to meet churches that are alive with spiritual freshness. The vitality in so many churches across the country is one of the most stirring signs of all that the tide is turning.

4. The Bible is once again a central focus

In the glory days of the '50s when one new suburban church after another rose up from a vacant field and its pews were quickly filled, there was an inglorious lacuna in the seemingly jam-packed life of a typical congregation. There was neither depth nor height. Instead of transforming the one-dimensional culture around them, the churches mirrored it. Activity there was in rich supply, but little reflection or meditation, little preaching about a world beyond this one, little to suggest Christianity offered more than a moral veneer. Is it puzzling that the '60s revolt against the social establishment tore off the veneer and threw it away?

Although that revolt caused churches to suffer a cataclysmic collapse of memberships and saw clergy, monks, nuns, and lay workers finding new meaning in secular service, it was not without blessing. As experience confirms, human necessity can become divine opportunity, and the churches' need drove them to search their own souls.

One result is a renewal of the Bible as the rule and fountain of faith. Historically, no Christian revival has ever been possible without Christians focusing attention on the scriptures as the source from which they must draw their inspiration and their edification.

All denominations now make Bible study as common a feature of their programs as quilting used to be. In Roman Catholic parish programs, the Bible features no less strongly than in Protestant churches.

Although different denominations and individuals understand biblical authority differently and interpret the Bible's contents differently, the churches are evidencing the common result of Christians going back to studying the Bible. They become infused with a sense of mission, gain identity as people with a message to share, and start to grow once they start to share that message. However inward may be the desire that takes people into small groups and opens the Bible in their hands, the ultimate result is to make them outward bound.

5. Experience in mission leads to the conviction that the church is about mission

Christians can indulge themselves for long periods as people who are at ease in Zion, comfortably preoccupied by the day-to-day institutional life of the church with its round of parochial events at one level and policy resolutions at another, able to exclude growth from the agenda of parish and synod. But once the Bible becomes a priority, a shift becomes irresistible. Mission becomes central. This "mission mentality" has come in strongly on the '90s tide.

Canadian denominations have always had missionary service in their programs, have always drawn missionary funds from congregations, and have always sent out men and women with a missionary call. But personal involvement has become the new feature of mission. In growth churches, it is not unusual to meet men and women who have spent their annual summer holidays in a mission project, possibly in a developing country, possibly in an aboriginal community of the Canadian north, possibly in an inner-city neighbourhood, possibly right near home. Mission takes many forms: erecting a clinic or shelter or school, assisting a program as teachers or helpers, settling immigrants and refugees, offering a refuge from the cold to the homeless or a meal to the hungry.

Some of the participants have been young people, willing and able to devote some of their limited time and unlimited energy. But not all. Others have been seniors, whose often unlimited time compensates for limited energy. All have involved themselves, and from that involvement gained a concept of the church itself as mission itself, not merely an institution that supports missions. They have been able to contribute to the continuing interaction between mission and growth.

Conceiving the church as mission has even been an unforeseen by-product of the decline that began in the '60s. When most churches were crowded, it was easier to identify them with society itself, but more difficult to sense any significant difference between churchgoers and everyone else. But when the churches went into reverse gear, the need for mission became clear for all to see.

Just going to church became an act that set one apart, made one aware of belonging to a minority, drove one to ask why one was doing it when so many others were not. When the divine commission to spread the good news of the gospel featured in the answer, there followed a desire to share the blessing one had found through church. That is the process we have seen at work in growth churches we have visited, and the frequency of our finding it is a sign of the tide coming back in.

6. The laicizing of the church is leading to new growth

To be a layman is not to be uninformed, inexpert, and non-professional. The Greek word *laos* means people and quite clearly implies belonging to a people. The laity in the church are not spiritual dependents looking to clergy to care for them. The word laity is an identification label for the church as God's people on earth.

Baptism is initiation into the laity, the people of God. By virtue of their baptism, clergy continue to be members of the laity, but laity who have been chosen for a unique ministry. Their fellow laity who have not been ordained devote themselves to other ministries in church and world alike.

Traditional titles, vestments, and clerical clothes have suggested that the church is a two-tier class structure. But in a kind of after-shock following the upheaval of the '60s, that structure has been shaken. It is now accepted that to be a lay person is to have a ministry, that to be baptized is to have a vocation. Some Sunday leaflets now announce the names of a church's clergy but also state that the ministers include all the members. Ministry is the vocation of every Christian to share in the church's mission, a vocation primarily performed by Christians ministering together as the church.

Lay people take an increasing lead in worship. No longer vested to look like clergy, they read lessons, lead prayers, carry up the eucharistic elements, administer Holy Communion, and even preach. Many churches have worship committees that design the services. The experience of growth churches has shown how central worship has to be in today's church life, but to be today's worship it has to reflect bottom-up preparation. Just repeating a liturgy, whether traditional or contemporary, is not enough. Worship must arise from the worshippers themselves to be meaningful to them, and the ability of growth churches to make that happen is one reason for their growth.

Some churches encourage an additional form of lay participation — the testimonial. Before or after the sermon, a lay witness backs up the sermon message with a story of personal experience that shows how the God who was at work in the Bible is still at work in today's world. The testimony shows that the gospel is not mere clerical theorizing; faith has worked in a lay person's life.

When lay ministry is accepted, going to church is transformed. Worship is no longer an event at which most people are a mere audience. Instead they form a community of people. The result is a dynamism in worship that inspires service and leads to growth. Churches grow when clergy appreciate that their role is to help their fellow Christians serve as their fellow ministers.

Instead of threatening the clergy's status, lay ministry reinforces the clergy by surrounding them with co-workers. They are no less the hub of the wheel, but more so. When the rim is turning all the faster with enough spokes to strengthen it, the hub is spinning all the more.

7. Women are prominent among those leading growth churches forward

Laicizing the church has focused attention upon the role of women. Some denominations have concluded that women should also be ordained, but even in those that have not, there has been widespread affirmation of women leaders, most offices being opened to them apart from pastoring churches and presiding at the sacraments. At Sunday services, a woman may carry the cross, read a lesson, or administer the Holy Communion. Not long ago, some people bridled at women becoming ushers. Now most congregations recognize and are grateful for the leadership of women whose qualifications and experience are equal to any man's.

Some denominations have moved faster than others. The Anglican Church of Canada has ordained many women as priests and consecrated two women as bishops. The United Church has been headed by a woman as moderator. Everywhere women, no longer confined to the women's auxiliary, serve as church-wardens or elders or managers. Growth churches want to take advantage of every resource God supplies them. Can it be good stewardship to ignore half the human race as a resource?

8. The number of people seeking theological education and ordination is growing

In the '60s thousands of clergy, nuns, and other ministers renounced their vocations and reverted to lay status. Some renounced their faith altogether. It was as though men and women who had assumed they were locked in for life had discovered that the door was open and there was freedom on the other side.

However understandable, this exodus threatened disaster when the remaining clerical loyalists aged and died, and the future did not look promising for the churches. But two factors intervened.

One was the commitment of so many clergy and others who just carried on. Enough crew remained on board to keep the ship sailing, even though some wondered where it was heading.

The other was a totally unpredictable renewal of vocations. In the '70s theological colleges and seminaries filled up and have remained full. The challenge is now not to find clergy but to find places for all the people who want to be ordained. One reason for the flood of vocations was the admission of women into ministries such as the Anglican priesthood, and the other was the increase of vocations as a second career or even a third.

Women now form from 35% to 50% of the enrolment in Canada's leading theological colleges. But they are not only young women, freshly graduated from universities. Many have grown-up children and some are grandmothers. Men, too, are taking up theological education in middle age or retirement.

Theological education has also gained a depth that will contribute to the mission of the churches. In the '60s when everything seemed to be falling apart, theological education at four universities was ecumenized. At Montreal's McGill University, it was already being provided by a Faculty of Divinity that included church colleges, and this step was quickly followed by the uniting of previously separate colleges into the Atlantic School of Theology at Halifax, the Vancouver School of Theology, and the Toronto School of Theology. Cooperation would follow among church-related colleges in the University of Saskatchewan at Saskatoon, and in the University of Western Ontario at London, Ontario.

With all these people trained and ready to lead, the churches are prepared for growth.

9. Churches are leading the struggle for social justice

Christianity is not complete until it gives prominence to social justice. Within the churches there is a wide variety of interpretations of social justice. On questions like abortion, sexuality, and the status of women, Christians may take polar opposite positions. On others, such as poverty and homelessness, they speak with a united voice. In their choice of methods for pursuing social justice, there is also variety. Some believe in working for gradual reform; others are convinced that only social upheaval and restructuring will be enough. But part of the promise of recovery is the way most Canadian churches have accepted that the Christian vocation demands witness for social justice.

All the denominations participate. Roman Catholic and Protestant, evangelical and charismatic, conservative and liberal, local churches support food banks, open youth programs to the community, and provide overnight shelter for the homeless.

They also actively lobby governments on matters of policy. While some evangelicals once believed that political action might potentially dilute their gospel ministry, they are now informed and articulate before the political authorities. While the historic denominations once preferred to influence policy through an old boys' network, they now lobby governments openly and regularly.

Fewer and fewer Christians now assume that their faith is otherworldly, pointing believers beyond this life without serious concern for existence here and now. During all the years when denominational membership was waning, the churches were increasing their social witness. In a time of labyrinthine complexity, authorities were welcoming help where they could get it, and were giving the churches a more respectful hearing than their numbers might have seemed to warrant.

If a church grows but lacks a passion for social justice, it is like the shallow soil in one of Jesus' parables, where the seed shot up quickly but just as quickly died because its roots were not deep enough. Renewing the witness for social justice is another sign that the tide is coming in for the Canadian churches.

10. The initiative has shifted from denominational headquarters to local churches

Finally, recovery is heralded by the way local churches are gaining a new creativity and denominational headquarters are shifting away from dominance toward service.

Denominations are not about to disappear. Their ministry is critical now more than ever.

They can motivate local churches to "think growth" by publishing information, holding seminars, and providing consultants.

They can enable churches to fulfil their mission by making low-interest loans to congregations whose need for building expansion exceeds their financial resources.

They can educate clergy and lay people by supporting theological colleges and seminaries and providing a variety of other courses, so that churches are staffed by leaders academically and professionally qualified.

They can equip churches with Sunday school literature, liturgical resources, music for worship, books for study groups and libraries, software, and other materials.

They can represent church opinion to governments more effectively than a congregation usually can.

They can take clergy and people beyond their parochial limits into national and global relationships that enhance their view of Christianity in the world today.

They can provide a sense of the continuity of historical development that avoids the peril of leaping from biblical times to the present and back again without appreciating how God has been at work in church and world for two millennia in between.

By all these ways the denominations can serve their churches, but none of them requires the dominance that was once assumed. Technology, education, and communication now give local churches a scope they lacked when they had to depend on "the national office."

A church need not buy copies of its denominational hymn book when it often can take hymns from many sources and either photocopy the words or project them onto a screen for people to sing. Sunday schools are no longer bound by denominational curricula but can adopt material from a variety of sources. Clergy and lay leaders have access to information to an extent not previously contemplated.

But this freedom does not imply parochial mutiny. It simply reflects the age of choice in which we live. In fact, by gaining access to a larger world, Christian persons have gained a freedom that makes for growth in ways that dependence could not.

Church growth is always ultimately local growth. People are not won to Christianity by national campaigns, but by face-to-face ministries. Churches do not grow by adding large numbers, but by converting individuals and families — and that makes local resourcefulness the key to growth. When a congregation is free to be creative in ways that meet the needs of people it hopes to win, growth ensues. The new freedom of local churches to take initiative is thus another sign that the tide is turning for Canadian churches.

Epilogue

The secret of growth

It need not have shocked Canadian Christians in the '60s to recognize that their historic denominations were suffering unprecedented reversal. History shows that churches fall as well as rise. Neither should it challenge Christians now to accept the paradoxical message of history: recovery follows recession. Canadian Christianity is on the eve of revival. The signs of its coming are visible and invite us to live and work in joyful expectation of it.

Yet history is not the primary reason for this expectation.

As we have seen in the stories of so many churches across the land, the human reasons for growth are many. Christians always live as children of nature as well as people of grace. But when all the social, economic, and cultural factors have been gathered, analyzed, collated, and interpreted, the ultimate reason for the growth of Christianity is that God is working out his purpose.

Be it on the Corinthian coast in the first century or in a Canadian community on the eve of the twenty-first, the work of Christ advances because the living Christ is alive in believers ready to share Christ's gospel with others. The secret of Christian growth is always the secret of Christ himself, and it is faith in Christ that gives his people hope for the future.

Above any other accounting, this explains why Canadian churches are growing again — and, despite times of reversal, will continue to grow. The inspiring scenes and testimonials described in this book are but part of the beginning.

The growth of Christianity will conclude only when Christ comes again and his church claims the promise "that at the name of Jesus every knee shall bow and every tongue confess that Jesus Christ is Lord, to the glory of God the Father" (Phil. 2: 10–11).

To be with Christ in his church is to be on the winning side. Amen. Praise God!